Education and
the Mass Media
in the Soviet Union
and Eastern Europe

edited by
Bohdan Harasymiw

The fourth of eight volumes of papers from the first international conference sponsored by the American Association for the Advancement of Slavic Studies, British National Association for Soviet and East European Studies, British Universities Association of Slavists, and Canadian Association of Slavists.

General Editor: Roger E. Kanet

The Praeger Special Studies program—utilizing the most modern and efficient book production techniques and a selective worldwide distribution network—makes available to the academic, government, and business communities significant, timely research in U.S. and international economic, social, and political development.

Education and the Mass Media in the Soviet Union and Eastern Europe

PRAEGER SPECIAL STUDIES IN INTERNATIONAL POLITICS AND GOVERNMENT

Praeger Publishers   New York   Washington   London

Library of Congress Cataloging in Publication Data
Main entry under title:

Education and the mass media in the Soviet Union and Eastern Europe.

(Praeger special studies in international polotics and government)
    The fourth of eight volumes of papers from the first international
Slavic conference sponsored by the American Association for the
Advancement of Slavic Studies, and others, held in Banff, Canada,
in 1974.
    Includes index.
    1. Education—Russia—Congresses.   2. Mass media—Russia—
Congresses.   3. Press—Russia—Congresses.   I. Harasymiw,
Bohdan.   II. American Association for the Advancement of Slavic
Studies.
LA832.E2985   370'.947   75-19789
ISBN 0-275-56170-4

PRAEGER PUBLISHERS
111 Fourth Avenue, New York, N.Y. 10003, U.S.A.

Published in the United States of America in 1976
by Praeger Publishers, Inc.

Printed in the United States of America

The studies published in this volume are selected from among those presented at the First International Slavic Conference, held in Banff, Alberta, Canada, September 4-7, 1974. The conference, which was attended by approximately 1, 500 persons, was sponsored by the American Association for the Advancement of Slavic Studies, the British Universities Association of Slavists, the British National Association for Soviet and East Europe Studies, and the Canadian Association of Slavists. Although the sponsorship of the conference was limited to the four major English-speaking Slavic associations, attendance and participation were much broader and included numerous scholars from continental Western Europe, Asia, Africa, Latin America, and Oceania. In addition, a substantial number of scholars from the Soviet Union and East Europe participated in the deliberations of the conference.

Among the more than 250 papers presented at the conference, a relatively large number have been selected for publication in two series of conference volumes. Papers in the social sciences are included in the series of volumes being published by Praeger Publishers of New York and those in the humanities are appearing in the series of books being published by Slavica Publishers of Cambridge, Massachusetts.

As general editor of both the Praeger and Slavica series of Banff publications, I wish to express my sincere appreciation to all of the individuals and institutions who made the conference possible. This includes the numerous government and private organizations that provided financial assistance, the members of the International Planning Committee who prepared the conference, and the participants themselves. Finally, I wish to thank the editors of the individual volumes in the two series and the authors of the essays for their major contributions.

CONTENTS

0354087

103774

LIST OF TABLES

INTRODUCTION
Bohdan Harasymiw

This volume is concerned in various ways with ideas as a subject of public policy in the communist countries of East Europe and the Soviet Union. Its constituent essays deal with education, the mass media, and public opinion. Each says something important about this aspect of the relationship between society and politics in that part of the world. Furthermore, each indicates the comparability of social processes in both communist and Western systems, and the desirability of furthering our understanding of those processes through comparative rather than either contrastive or isolated case studies.

Oskar Anweiler discusses comparative education and area studies, and notes that the gap between them is being closed by the development of interdisciplinary studies in comparative communism. Both Eastern and Western scholars are, he says, approaching comparative education as a social science. This prepares the way for a new stage in research on comparative education in Eastern Europe and the Soviet Union. Communist scholars since the 1960s have begun to conduct research on education aimed at practical application in policymaking. They are studying each other's educational systems as well as foreign ones. This leads them, as it does their Western counterparts, in the direction of elaborating a model of the communist educational system. There are, however, some technical problems facing all who venture into this field. These difficulties include the absence of a general theory of the educational subsystem in a socialist society, as well as the search for common functional equivalents, a data base, and terminology. In addition, there are questions regarding the explanation of national differences in educational systems: Do cultural traditions play a role in the creation of the communist educational system? Are national differences withering away? What are the results of using education to create a new political culture?

There are, according to Anweiler, three types of models useful in explaining communist educational systems: (1) models dealing with the relationship between education and society; (2) models describing the functioning of the educational system; and (3) models relating education to learning. Of the first of these, the developmental and totalitarian models are often used for the USSR by Western scholars. Neither of these, however, is very suitable, for either the Soviet Union or Eastern Europe. The "transformational model," he says, may be better. Marxist-Leninist scholars, on the other hand, still carry out the study of education and society very formally. But they, too, will move toward more scientific models as the need in their countries for research-based planning in educational policy becomes more apparent.

xi

The second type of modeling is not yet being done by socialist scholars. Here, too, the demand for reliable knowledge and scientific understanding will impel them to go beyond formal description of educational systems to functional explanations based on comprehensive models. This need is particularly obvious where the aims and operation of education diverge. For example, equality of educational opportunity is a common principle in the socialist countries, but economic requirements have led to significant changes in the educational structure away from this principle. Thus, the comprehensive or unified school system yields to a differentiated one, and equality of opportunity is violated. A comparative study—whether it aims at redirecting policy or simply understanding the system—should, therefore, not just juxtapose forms of differentiation but also give a functional explanation of the differentiation.

The third type of model endeavors to ascertain the contribution of education to personality development. This is also an important area of research. It has to be studied through comparative curriculum research. Again, however, a multidimensional modeling is needed.

All three types of models are relevant to educational policymaking in the Soviet Union and Eastern Europe. They also are relevant for Western scholars. By studying education in the socialist countries, the latter can, among other things, contribute to the discussion of educational-social matters in their own countries as well as to educational planning and reform.

Elizabeth Koutaissoff asks in her essay about the aim of public education. Traditionally, it has been treated in the USSR as a means of manpower training. There is, however, another perspective: that of the consumers of education. This stresses human development. From this viewpoint, the Soviet government, no less than its counterparts in other industrialized countries, may be seen as treating human beings as mere factors of production. But even in the Soviet Union, where manpower planning is institutionalized and geared to the state's needs, the career aspirations of youths are now being studied. Results of the studies pose great problems for the planners, problems of reconciling public and private needs.

Soviet sociological studies indicate that youths prefer intellectual to manual occupations. In one sense this is good, for it falls into line with the state's search for talent to be developed as specialized manpower and to promote scientific progress. But for the production of the nonspecialist labor force, this is a problem. There is a shortage of juvenile labor because of young people remaining in school. When they graduate, they are educated but unskilled. That, too, is a problem. Yet the personal wishes of young people for education do have to be taken into account. To this end, educational institutions are being upgraded; vocational schools are adding academic study to practical; the professional-technical schools are being converted to secondary schools from which students can advance to higher education; and

teachers' qualifications are being improved. But the personal drive for
more education, and at the most prestigious institutions, results in
great competitiveness as well as great imbalances between aptitudes
and vocations. Vocational guidance is therefore a very prominent concern in Soviet education. Beyond the practical, however, the Soviets
are seriously grappling, as Koutaissoff shows, with the theoretical
study of matching occupations and aptitudes generally in the labor force
so as to reconcile the fundamental problem of public versus private
needs in a more satisfactory way than hitherto. In this way, she concludes, "the search to adapt work to man rather than to allow him to
remain 'an appendage of the machine' has definitely started."

George Avis reports that the vocational orientations of students in
higher education are a source of concern to Soviet authorities. From his
review of Soviet sociological studies of higher education, he finds that
"many secondary school graduates regard higher education and student
status as an end in itself, a social value to be consumed, rather than
as preparation for a specific occupation." These studies show that students are not well acquainted with their future specialty. Genuine vocational orientations, therefore, seem absent in course selection. The
result, not surprisingly, is that many students "reject their specialty
as a career." This, of course, has practical as well as ideological
implications.

Also having similar implications is the whole question of the relationship between social class and access to higher education, which
Avis examines in his essay. There is indeed a relationship, one that
may be summed up as intelligentsia self-recruitment. Soviet sociologists, however, see the inequalities of access as economic and liable
to wither away. Yet, notes Avis, their preoccupation and dismay with
this situation are difficult to explain: In spite of the theoretical ration-
alizations, there is deep concern. The whole situation shows, Avis
says, that there are some sociopsychological phenomena in this area
that are not amenable to scientific social control. In the event, the
Soviets are debating two different approaches to the problem of class
bias in higher education: One is to regulate recruitment; the other, not
to. The debate underscores the basic fact that Soviet higher education
is characterized by functional contradictions that need to be recognized
by the Soviets before they can be resolved. Their problem, that of
"warming up" demand for higher education among the talented, but also
"cooling down" demand from the less talented and avoiding disappointment for them, is one common to other modern industrialized nations.
It is a public policy problem for which interdisciplinary research rather
than ideology alone may have some answers.

The totalitarian model of the communist political system has emphasized the importance of ideology and its pervasiveness in both policy
and political behavior. The first three essays in this volume show,
however, that ideology is not so pervasive or exclusive in research on
educational policy, at least in the Soviet Union. The next three essays

likewise indicate that the flow of ideas and information in communist systems is neither so uniform nor so unidirectional as the totalitarian conception had led one to believe. Rather, there are gatekeepers and opinion leaders with a surprisingly wide access to diverse kinds of information. These custodians, therefore, have a key role in the dissemination of ideas among the public, but they are not the politicians and what they inject into the media of mass communication is not always in keeping with official ideology.

Alexandra Kwiatkowski, for instance, examines nonconformist trends in the Soviet journal, Novy mir. Nonconformism, she says, "involves being anti-Stalinist, critical, polemic, and sometimes challenging acts and principles of the establishment." For this, the journal has been criticized by Pravda and Literaturnaia gazeta. Sometimes it has refused to conform to official demands; on other occasions, it has submitted. Its writers have endeavored to escape criticism through the use of Aesopian language as well as expression by subterfuge in the manner of Montesquieu's Lettres persanes. The unanswered question is whether its readers have been able to follow these subterfuges.

At any rate, official policy regulating the expression of ideas in the USSR is not without openly expressed dissent. There is no finality to it; it is discussed by those in society who feel most affected by it. Mme. Kwiatkowski sums up the attitude of the nonconformist intellectuals as being opposed to: incompetence, dogmatism, inefficiency and political subjugation of the mass media, the sham of elections and the regime's arbitrariness, and high living on the part of officials and their own opposition to progress. One contributor to Novy mir is quoted as complaining about "mass communications that do not communicate with anybody except professional politicians." Others have protested indirectly about the trial of intellectuals for their opinions. In general, Mme. Kwiatkowski offers us an interesting picture of the relations of Soviet intellectuals and politicians, each with their respective eternal preoccupations: truth and power.

Theodore Kruglak presents an account of the development of news agencies in the socialist countries of Europe, another aspect of governmental regulation of information and ideas. Although for different reasons, these agencies are, like their pre-communist predecessors, state-controlled. The most interesting aspect of their relationships within the bloc is that the smaller "national" agencies of Eastern Europe are not dominated by their bigger "international" brother, TASS. This is true because of: (1) the emergence of Hsin Hua (New China News Agency) as an international agency and because the Eastern Europeans have . agreements with it; (2) the use of dispatches from other agencies; and (3) the fact that national (as opposed to international) agencies are now more viable as news gatherers. So the socialist countries' agencies are not bound to TASS. Of course, within these countries the newspaper editor is limited and relies mainly on his national agency for foreign news. But the agency foreign editor is in a different position, very similar to his Western counterpart. His sources are many, and he truly acts the same role as the latter: that of gatekeeper. What differentiates the two is their concept of news. Still, their function is comparable, despite their own ideology or that of the observer.

Michel Kwiatkowski elaborates on the operation of one East European news agency, that of Yugoslavia. Here we have a case study of the domestic relationship between government and agency. Not that Tanjug is typical of Eastern European agencies: it is operated by self-management; it has no monopoly because Yugoslav papers do have correspondents abroad; and, like its national foreign policy, it is nonaligned. Yet it does illustrate how news is managed in one communist one-party state. The agency's structure allows for some formal political independence. Since 1974, with the inclusion of more official representatives in its governing body, governmental control has become greater. Another source of influence on the agency is the Yugoslav Communist League: the director and some employees are members; the Party's Central Committee is an important customer. The agency therefore has two modes of operation. In the normal one it is like any foreign agency, exerting an influence on public opinion through the selection of news (gatekeeping). While it is quite frank, incidentally, with news from other socialist countries, it is not always so with domestic Yugoslav news. In a crisis, it is liable to be subjected to influence through pressure from the politicians. Tanjug's news policy is therefore squeezed between professional objectivity and political subordination. In Kwiatkowski's view, however, the Yugoslav journalists have struck a balance between political pressure and professional conscientiousness.

Kwiatkowski believes that Tanjug has a margin of freedom unlike other Eastern European agencies; it could evolve toward greater objectivity with each period of political thaw. It seems to me that this would bring the informed public closer to public policy. This broadening of participation in the policy process, of course, requires some reconceptualization of politics on the part of the power holders in this as in any other communist system. Such a reconceptualization appears to be under way in the USSR.

Georges Mink examines the Soviet official attitude to and conceptualization of public opinion surveys. His investigation shows that "the utility of social research is now recognized by central authority." The reconceptualization has involved treating public opinion not as something to be shaped but rather as something to be discerned, studied, determined. The danger of not knowing the public mood was apparently brought home to the Soviets by the Polish events of 1970-71. The recognition of the autonomy of public opinion and the usefulness of studying it bodes well, Mink notes, for social research. One might add that it is also significant for the conduct of the political process. Nevertheless, Soviet scholars still entertain an ambiguity in their approach to public opinion because of an awareness of what it (ideologically) "should" be. The idea of a "socialist public"—between individual opinion and mass conformity to ideology, between individualism and social "unity" of opinion—has been put forward. Yet empirical studies have shown instead a great diversity of opinions among the public on many important questions.

The sanctioning of public opinion surveys, of course, grants a certain legitimacy to independent public opinion itself. Indeed, as Mink concludes, there is already an acknowledgment that public opinion polls are needed to facilitate the exercise of political power. (This, incidentally, carries us back to the theme of educational policy and young people's expectations.) "There is increasing pressure," Mink states, "to give due consideration to the link between holding power and the opinion of those under it." For the observer attuned to discerning at least the political significance of phenomena, this appears to sum up well an overriding theme in the essays in the present volume: the interaction between the individual, the state, society, and ideas.

Education and the Mass Media in the Soviet Union and Eastern Europe

**TOWARD A COMPARATIVE STUDY
OF THE EDUCATIONAL SYSTEMS
IN THE SOCIALIST COUNTRIES
OF EUROPE: RECENT
FINDINGS AND PROBLEMS**
Oskar Anweiler

FROM AREA STUDIES IN EDUCATION TOWARD
COMPARATIVE ANALYSIS

Comparative Education and Communist Studies
in Western Countries

It may be said with some justification that the development of
comparative education as a discipline of educational sciences and, on
the other hand, the development of area studies on Eastern Europe and
the Soviet Union proceeded in two separate ways. Notwithstanding the
fact that some of the pioneers of comparative education, such as I.
Kandel, N. Hans, and S. Hessen, because of their origin and their
special interests, devoted themselves to the problems of Russian and
Soviet education, their works had no influence on area studies, which
expanded quickly after 1945. That kind of research was mainly a domain of historians and social scientists. On the other hand, some
remarkable studies of political and social scientists concerned with
problems of education in the Soviet Union and Eastern Europe (for
example, political education) remained outside the discussion on
methodological questions in comparative education. In some respect
this situation reflected the well-known and often criticized lack of
communication between area specialists and social or educational
scientists in general.

Now it seems that, in connection with the endeavors to develop
a new interdisciplinary field of studies and research, comparative
studies of communism, a new stage in research about educational

This essay was previously published in <u>Comparative Education</u>
11, no. 1 (1975): 3-11, and is reprinted with permission.

problems in Eastern Europe also can be achieved. As far as I can see, the idea behind comparative communist studies is threefold: first, the former separation of area studies and the related disciplines (economics, law, sociology) can be overcome by a higher level of theoretical consideration and the application of methods used in the "mother disciplines" for the regional studies; second, there is a move toward an inter- or multidisciplinary approach in research based on a common search for models as instruments for analysis and prognosis; third, the comparative method can be used in a more strict and obvious way than up to now. "Familiarity with the comparative method would help scholars to make significant contributions to knowledge of specific areas and to the ongoing efforts to improve the generalizations of comparative theory."[1]

A similar development has occurred within comparative education. The former kind of studies concerned with one educational system or treating a group of educational systems in a purely descriptive manner has given way to the problem approach, to problem-oriented, cross-national comparative studies. Even more radical proposals aim at a highly formalized comparison of at least two units. "A comparative study is essentially an attempt as far as possible to replace the names of systems (countries) by the names of concepts (variables)."[2] In such a methodological concept, the former area approach has lost its significance even with the presupposition of comparison as the final step.

One cannot follow such ideas here, but it seems to be a general result of recent developments in comparative education, as well as in the comparative studies of communism, that in the future emphasis will be put mainly on cross-national comparative studies of selected problems in education in socialist (communist) countries.[3] We should like to make a further distinction: Studies concerned with comparison between the different socialist (communist) systems should be called "cross-communist" comparative studies; comparisons made between socialist/communist systems and other societies (Western, developing countries) we should like to call cross-societal.[4] This essay is concerned with the first kind of problems only.

Comparative studies of communism are devoting themselves a great deal to the Soviet and Chinese variations. In comparative education, so far there are only first attempts to compare in detail Chinese and Soviet education.[5] We discuss here only the problems of comparative studies of socialist educational systems in Europe (of course including the whole Soviet Union). The research work done in this field by Western scholars (first attempts of a general survey, problem-oriented comparisons, and methodological reflections) provides the basis for our outline as well as for the recent discussions within the field of comparative education in the socialist countries themselves.

Comparative Educational Studies
in the Socialist Countries

The discipline of comparative education has established itself as a distinct field of research and as an academic subject in the USSR, Poland, the German Democratic Republic (GDR), Czechoslovakia, and other Eastern European countries only since the beginning of the 1960s. What has been tried is to trace back a Marxist comparative education to the beginning of the twentieth century, and one can find first attempts at a comparison between the newly created educational system in Soviet Russia and the capitalist world in the 1920s, but on the whole comparative education, based on the principles of Marxism-Leninism, came into existence only in the period of increased international communication between the socialist countries and the West. During the rather short period of its development, the discipline passed through the stages familiar to West European and American history of comparative education: At the beginning there was a rather superficial interest in foreign education, followed by a more serious and systematic study of educational systems in several countries. At present the move toward problem-oriented, cross-national studies, especially to cross-societal (socialist system versus capitalist) can be noticed. Marxist-Leninist comparative education has made use, at least to some degree, of the methodological discussions that have taken place in the West. There are authors who have assumed the basic technical instruments of research work without ideological scruples. Others have disguised the adapted assumptions to adopt them into the official system of ideology and pursued their task in a more polemical manner. [6]

The proclaimed official foundation being the principles of Marxism-Leninism produces different results as far as research work is concerned. From the political viewpoint, comparative education in socialist countries has to fulfill a defensive and offensive function against "bourgeois" education. By the way, such expectations often create a very uncomfortable position for people engaged in this field. They must prove their loyalty to the system and legitimate their activity by occasional attacks against their counterparts in Western countries. The ideological bias that often can be noticed of some comparative educationists, namely in the USSR and GDR, is to some degree also a response to rather polemical attitudes on the part of Western comparativists in the past.

More important for the practical function of comparative education in socialist countries is another task. The results of research should contribute to the planning and developing of their own educational system. Material collected on foreign education should be utilized to support educational policy decision making and for the solution of particular problems. Therefore, documentation on foreign education

plays an important part in the departments of comparative education in
the respective research institutes. Such concentration on "practical
questions" is not without negative effects on long-term planning in
research, and creates restrictions on a broader concept of basic
research. There still seems to be a shortage of qualified research personnel with a broader theoretical foundation and, again mainly in the
USSR and the GDR, with some experience of studies conducted abroad.

The Impact of Recent Educational Reforms
and of Educational Planning on
Comparative Educational Studies in Socialist Countries

During the educational reforms in the Soviet Union and in Eastern
Europe since 1958, comparative studies or arguments deriving from an
international comparison have played different roles at various times.
So far as we know, there was little regard to international educational
developments in the period of the Khrushchev reform (1958-64) in the
USSR, but a growing interest after the reform in the schools, which
worked between 1964 and 1966, also took into consideration experience
abroad. But in connection with the influence that Khrushchev's program
of polytechnical reform exerted on the school reform in the other socialist countries, there have been written the first comparative surveys
on the development and different practices of polytechnization. [7] In the
German Democratic Republic, the planning of the new unified system
of education, which found expression in the law of 1965, also had some
influence on comparative studies. The project on "Unity and Differentiation in the Educational System" was a result of the political interest
in that central question of school reform. [8]
Results of cross-national studies and international surveys of
modern educational problems have been incorporated into the research
process, and to some degree even into political decisions in Poland.
Polish educationalists frequently discussed methodological questions
of comparative education, earlier than their colleagues in other socialist
countries. [9] During the preparation of the new program for educational
reform, confirmed by the Sejm in October 1973, some institutes and
research groups were engaged in studies with a comparative problem
approach. [10]
Since the beginning of the 1970s, a clear shift of interest and
research policy can be recognized. In connection with the program of
closer cooperation and integration within Comecon under the leadership
of the Soviet Union, there is a remarkable trend toward greater collaboration in education, too. The ministries of education and other official
institutions and research institutes are developing a system of permanent mutual contacts, an exchange of information, and research planning
programs in education. For the first time, the educational systems of

the socialist countries are thus becoming an object of comparative
study and evaluation on a broad scale.

The theoretical foundation of this move toward the creation of a
new type of supranational Marxist comparative education can be seen
in the assumed principle of "general laws" in the development of the
socialist societies, which is applied in the educational field, too. In
this perspective, the common features of a socialist educational system, culminating in the idea of a communist educative society, gradually drive back the still persisting "national pecularities." Of course,
there will exist some distinctions in the structure of the educational
system even in the communist future, but they are looked upon as minor
modifications of the generally valid and approved model of a communist
educational system. The most important future task of comparative education as a science, therefore, lies in the elaboration of such a model. [11]

IN SEARCH OF AN ANALYTICAL FRAMEWORK

Technical Problems

Sometimes the more technical problems of research are neglected
when methodological discussions on a rather abstract level are occupying the field. But as experience proves, such questions must be taken
up in order to avoid mistakes in cross-communist comparative studies.

Looking after relevant problems in a group of educational systems
to be studied in a comparative way, one needs a prior agreement about
the scope and main characteristic features of what is called the "educational system." In connection with the theoretical preliminary studies
in Poland mentioned above, it has proven necessary to define the central terms used in administrative and political practice and in educational theory. [12] As before in the GDR and USSR, systems analysis
has been made use of to some degree, defining the educational system
as a subsystem of society. But there is still a marked lack of a general
theory of the educational system in a socialist society based on comparative studies. The common conviction seems to be that the educational system—that is, organized learning and the education processes
outside of schools under public control—should be part of an overall
"educative society."

As long as there persist different organizational structures in the
socialist educational systems (length of schooling, types of schools,
final examinations at different levels), the problem of functional equiv-
alence is of great importance for comparative analysis. It is a "technical" problem insofar as common criteria must be applied for a necessary
classification that enables comparison. Neither in the socialist countries nor by Western researchers has there been developed up to now

such a nomenclature that is comprehensive and flexible enough to cover the different elements of the educational systems in order to make them comparable. In theory, it should be much easier for the socialist countries to come to an agreement on such questions than within the heterogeneous international organizations like UNESCO.

A second technical problem of great importance is the construction of a data base appropriate to comparative work. It is well known that in some socialist countries figures are published only very fragmentarily, and the materials at our disposal are quite incomplete. But even the officially published data are mostly without the necessary explanation concerning the criteria applied, the methods of collection, and the sample. It is evident that in such cases statistical comparisons between the educational systems are almost an adventure. During recent years there has been some improvement in that field, due mainly to research by sociologists in the respective countries. However, compared with the abundance of educational statistical data in most Western countries, the basis for a detailed quantitative educational comparison among the socialist states is still limited.

A third problem, already touched on, is that of educational terminology used in the different countries, and together with it the question of translation in comparative investigations. It is of course no technical problem, strictly speaking. The question is not mainly that of appropriate translations of school types, teaching subjects, and administrative designations, although such questions are sometimes difficult enough. Behind the technical problem of more or less well-defined educational terminology and adequate translation, lies the deeper problem of hermeneutic approach (verstehen) as a method of cross-cultural comparisons. Every investigation of the present educational systems in Eastern Europe that takes into account their historical past and the philosophical background of the educational theory, finds itself confronted with questions of that kind. Therefore, it seems a basic requirement for comparative researchers is to develop competencies such as learning the language, culture, and history of the society of which education is a part.

National and Cultural Diversity Versus Common Political and Ideological Objectives

Comparative educationists in the past often used the model of "national character" to explain the characteristic features of a nation's educational system. In the meantime, cultural anthropology as well as other social sciences proved nearly unanimously that global explanations of that kind are worthless and lack empirical evidence. Nevertheless the question remains to what degree the cultural traditions of a nation are playing an important role in the process of building up a socialist/communist society, including a new system of education. The general assumption of the Marxist-Leninist comparative education we mentioned about—the "withering away" of national pecularities within the socialist camp—is unsatisfactory because the empirical evidence still gives insufficient support for such a thesis.

In searching for an analytical framework, we must recognize a possible dual approach to our problem. One who is mostly interested in philosophical or political aspects of Marxist-Leninist education in East European countries will find sufficient material in official proclamations, textbooks, and curriculums which may confirm the view of dominating common features in education and the persistence of only minor differences in the particular country. But if one is asking whether such general principles are realized in the educational process and what the conditions are under which educational practice operates he, of course, will find more differences on many points. Comparative survery of the Eastern European educational systems written by Western authors in the 1960s underlined, besides some basic common trends, a broad range of national variations in structure, planning, and classroom teaching. [13]

For a cross-national analysis from an educational point of view it is decisive to understand the real educational meaning of a problem treated in a comparative way. The problem of polytechnical education may serve as an example. Polytechnical education belongs to the core educational program of Marxist-Leninist theory and practice of education. During the history of Soviet education, and during the educational developments in Eastern Europe since the end of the 1940s, there have been very different approaches to realizing the general principles of polytechnical education. The main task of a historical and comparative study of the attempts of polytechnization would be to identify the different didactic concepts behind the practical measures and to investigate the different conditions (economic, social, cultural), which were more favorable in some countries than in others. The purpose of cross-national analysis of polytechnical education is to contribute to a model of technical education in modern societies. The national variations are in this respect only of interest for the theory of education insofar as they indicate the variety of possible solutions. [14]

The second example aims at showing the possible contribution of cross-communist educational studies to comparative studies of communism in general. The educational systems in Eastern Europe and East Germany were transformed in the late 1940s and early 1950s according to the type of Soviet education of that time. The notion of "Sovietization", which has been applied to this transformation by Western authors, is of course denied by the official view in the socialist states. But nevertheless it remains an important question that can be treated only in a comparative way: By which means and with what results has education been used to create a new political culture in societies with very different traditions?

A special question for such studies is, for example, the approach used in attempts to introduce the program of "socialist patriotism and proletarian internationalism" into school curriculums and extracurricular activities. Here again, the officially proclaimed intentions must be checked by empirical evidence as far as possible. A comparative study should take into account the development of a kind of communist national consciousness in the different Eastern European states, which may have some effects on the educational area. Unfortunately Marxist-Leninist comparative education does not and cannot contribute to research on such problems because they are politically inopportune.

Models of Explanation

Comparative education in Western countries is now more and more concerned with problems of theory building, making use of vast materials and statistical data produced by empirical findings. A similar trend can be noted in socialist countries. The discussion of epistemological problems of educational research in the Soviet Union, namely about "logic" and "history," also have had some influence on the theory of comparative education. [15] Like Western social and educational scientists, Marxist scholars stress the necessity to create and apply models for the explanation of the development, structure, and functioning of social systems. The use of models in cross-national educational research, including cross-communist comparisons, promises progress in our field.

A model may be defined in a formal way as a theoretical construct of interdependent elements, containing a kind of abstract reality. Its purpose is to explain complex social phenomena by reducing them to a "system" according to definite, applied rules. Considering cross-communist educational studies, there can be distinguished three kinds of models: (1) models to explain the relations and the interdependence of education and society (structure and development); (2) models to explain the functions of the different parts of an educational system; and (3) models to explain the interdependence of the educational system and learning-teaching processes.

EDUCATIONAL SYSTEM AND SOCIETY

The first type of model belongs to macrosociological patterns that seek to explain the relation between society and the educational system in a larger sense. With regard to the Soviet Union, Western scholars have often used the development model, and there is sufficient proof for the correlation of educational policy and the modernization of Russia to make sense in using such a model. [16] A second general concept, totalitarianism, played an important part because of its function as a model of demarcation from Western democracies during the 1950s; it seemed suitable in education to stress the ideological indoctrination of youth as the main feature of communist education.

For a cross-communist comparison, neither concept is very suitable. The development model, which describes the socioeconomic change of a formerly predominantly agrarian society, cannot be applied to Czechoslovakia or East Germany, and only to a small degree to Poland. The criticism of the totalitarian model has sufficiently proved that it represented a theoretically uncontrolled mixture of political evaluation and historical and empirical facts. More suitable for comparative purposes may perhaps be the still theoretical and not further elaborated transformation model, when applied to the Eastern European countries after 1945. The "revolution from outside," which exposed those countries to a radical and deliberate transformation of society, gave high priority to educational policy. The transformation model belongs to the recently advocated studies of comparative political culture. [17] The last concept to be mentioned is that of the industrial society, sometimes connected with the convergence theory. The notion of industrial society embraces socialist and capitalist systems, and the concept is therefore rejected by Marxist-Leninist social sciences, including comparative education. Because this model does not belong primarily to cross-communist studies, we shall not discuss it here. [18]

When discussing relations between education and society in socialist countries, Marxist-Leninist comparative education usually does so in a very formal way. The starting point is the statement that socialist societies are moving toward the next stage of development, communism, according to "historical laws," and therefore the educational system is following the same path. Up to now there have been very few attempts—based on empirical materials and employing a system of categories—to analyze the relationship between educational development and society in detail. The facts usually referred to, such as the end of illiteracy, the creation of a unified school system, the prolongation of school attendance, and the policy of social equalization of access to education, are taken as evidence for the progress of socialist societies. But what remains undiscussed is the question of the special character of interdependence between education and society in socialist countries—based upon empirical data, and integrated into a general model.

But one can foresee that the necessity to elaborate such models will increase to the same extent as educational planning and scientific research on social systems prognostication are based on hypotheses with the purpose of offering alternatives. The already mentioned expert committee for educational reform in Poland and some other research and planning groups have started to work according to this principle. It seems to be one of the advantages of socialist systems that there is the possibility of modeling the future educational system as part of the planned progress of the whole society. For a comparative analysis,

it may therefore be meaningful to start with the objectives proclaimed,
then to list the measures undertaken to attain the different aims, and
lastly to confront them with the results after a reasonable period. A
pattern of this kind could help to evaluate the real progress of the different educational systems according to their own principles and values.

FUNCTIONS AND STRUCTURE OF THE EDUCATIONAL SYSTEM

The second type of model we propose for the purpose of cross-
communist analysis relates to the internal structure of the educational
system and its functions. We already possess a number of surveys
prepared by institutes in some socialist countries, describing the organizational structure of the school system and of vocational training,
as well as some special problems in the individual socialist countries,
with a comparative intent. In fact, they are mostly juxtapositions of
the different types and forms of schooling and training, without a comparative analysis of the functions that the respective institutions fulfill.
A pure description of the officially proclaimed tasks of the educational
institutions is nearly useless because the real function for the society
or the individual person may differ strongly.

So far, comparative studies undertaken in the socialist countries
have not attempted to construct a general model applicable to a different
educational system in more than a formal way. Such a model should be
multidimensional; that is, it must correlate (1) the guiding principles
of the educational system, (2) its organizational structure, and (3) the
functions of the system's elements. For example, all socialist educational systems are governed by the principle of equality of educational
opportunity; therefore, the comprehensive (unified) school system belongs to the articles of faith of socialist educational policy. Nevertheless, other important factors, mainly economic, exercise considerable
influence on the structure of the educational system. The principle of
comprehensiveness is therefore questioned by other considerations,
which may lead to a more differentiated system of schooling. As a
result of differentiation in various forms, including special schools
for mathematics or language training, the general principle of equal
educational opportunity may be violated to an extent that creates new
social problems. Therefore, comparative study analyzing the functions
of differentiation within the school system should not be restricted to
a formal juxtaposition of the various methods and forms of differentiation.

CONCEPTS OF TEACHING AND CURRICULUMS

The third kind of model to be used for the purpose of comparative analysis is connected with the relations between the educational system and teaching. With the already quoted exception of polytechnical education, comparative studies on special fields of learning and of school curriculums covering more than one socialist country are still to be produced. Again, the concept for such a comparative analysis must be modeled multidimensionally. The analysis of foreign language teaching, for example, in several East European countries must take into account at least the following elements: (1) the traditional role of a certain foreign language in the given society and the new importance of Russian as the officially favored language in most countries; (2) the role (scope, length, examination importance) that language studies play within the study programs; (3) the importance ascribed to a foreign language after completion of formal schooling (as in professional life); (4) methods of instruction in foreign languages; (5) the contents of textbooks; (6) the level of teacher training and competence; and (7) the opportunity to come into contact with native speakers.

As the example shows, the problem of comparative analysis of a given teaching subject in different school systems is related to many factors outside the school. So-called didactic models therefore are not pure formalizations of what is going on in classrooms but broader concepts of interrelationships between school and society focused in one special field of learning. The program of comparative curriculum research put forward recently, [19] therefore, seems to offer additional possibilities for a deeper understanding of socialist educational systems.

It should be mentioned that at present the question of personality development plays an important role in the educational theory of socialist countries. The problem is related to the theory of general socialist education (sozialistische Allgemeinbildung) and to collective education, too. Psychology, sociology, and philosophy are requested to contribute, as well as the different branches of education. [20] Marxist-Leninist comparative education is engaged only to a minor degree in this area because of the conviction that the theoretical principles and even the educational methods to be used for the achievement of the common aims are of general value and must not be treated in respect to the different national conditions. Concerning Western comparativists, it should be a noteworthy task to take up the discussion with representatives of socialist education on principal questions of this kind.

CONCLUSIONS

Comparative educationists in the West who study the educational systems of socialist countries are often regarded by the other side with suspicion. Besides a sometimes justifiable criticism on the approach in research work done in the past, an ideological and even national bias also plays a role. The officially maintained view is that cross-communist comparative research is so closely linked with politics that any attempt to develop an empirical research program of this kind on a broader scale, including cooperation with the respective research groups in socialist countries, seems doubtful in the near future. Western scholars thus are usually excluded from direct participation in studies conducted in the socialist countries.

Nevertheless, they may contribute to comparative studies of the kind we have discussed in different ways. First, they should evaluate, and criticize if necessary, methods of research and presentation of results of comparative studies produced by Marxist-Leninist comparative education. Second, they should take up questions in their own research activities that are neglected or only treated insufficiently in the socialist research programs. Third, they should introduce the results of comparative studies on socialist education into the general discussion within the educational and social sciences and into educational planning and reforms in their own countries.

NOTES

1. Helen Desfosses Cohn, "Comparative Communism and Comparative Studies: A Note on Shared Concerns," Newsletter on Comparative Studies of Communism 6, no. 4 (1973): 5.

2. Harold J. Noah, "Defining Comparative Education: Conceptions," in Relevant Methods in Comparative Education, ed. Reginald Edwards et al. (Hamburg: UNESCO Institute for Education, 1973), p. 114. ·

3. As far as the socialist countries call their systems socialist, this label can be used; on the other hand, it seems appropriate to speak of communist systems, even in terms of the ideology of Marxism-Leninism.

4. There is still a lack of common usage of terms like cross-national, cross-cultural, and cross-societal. In other languages (such as German and French), the terminology is even more complicated. The distinctions read in German: intra-kommunistischer Vergleich ("cross-communist comparison") and inter-systemarer Vergleich ("cross-societal comparison").

5. R. F. Price, "Labour and Education in Russia and China," Comparative Education 10, no. 1 (1974): 13-23.

6. Friedrich W. Busch, "Zur Konzeption einer Marxistischen Vergleichenden Padagogik, " Bildung und Erziehung 24, no. 6 (1971): 540-50. Werner Kienitz, "On the Marxist Approach to Comparative Education in the German Democratic Republic, " Comparative Education 7, no. 1 (1971): 21-31.

7. Das Schulwesen sozialistischer Lander in Europa, ed. Deutsches Padagogisches Zentralinstitut (Berlin, 1962); Mieczyslaw Pecherski and Antoni Taton, Wiez szkoly z zyciem w krajach socjalistycznych (Warsaw: Panstwowe Zaklady Wydawnictw Szkolnych, 1963).

8. Einheitlichkeit und Differenzierung. Ein internationaler Vergleich, ed. Werner Kienitz et al. (Berlin: Volk und Wissen, 1971).

9. Bogdan Suchodolski, "O zagadnieniach i zadaniach pedagogiki porownawczej, " Zarys pedagogiki, vol. 1 (3rd ed. ; Warsaw, 1964); Marian Wachowski, "Przedmiot pedagogiki porownawczej, " Kwartalnik pedagogiczny 10, no. 1 (1965): 49-71; T. J. Wiloch, Wprowadzenie do pedagogiki porownawczej, (Warsaw: Panstwowe Wydawnictwo Naukowe, 1970); Bogdan Nawroczynski, "Przedmiot i metoda pedagogiki porownawczej, " Studia z pedagogiki porownawczej (Studia pedagogiczne, vol. 26) (Wroclaw: Wydawnictwo Polskiej Akademii Nauk, 1972).

10. The report of the Expert Committee for the Elaboration of a Report on the Situation of Education in the People's Republic of Poland under the chairmanship of Jan Szczepanski appeared under the title Raport o stanie oswiaty w PRL (Warsaw: Panstwowe Wydawnictwo Naukowe, 1973); see the abridged version in Nowa szkola, no. 4 (1973).

11. See Werner Kienitz, "Einige theoretische Fragen der Entwicklung der Vergleichenden Padagogik als Wissenschaftsdisziplin, " Vergleichende Padagogik 8, no. 4 (1972): 368-90; M. A. Sokolowa, "Uber allgemeine Gesetzmassigkeiten und nationale Besonderheiten in der Entwicklung der Volksbildung der sozialistischen Lander Europas, " Vergleichende Padagogik 9, no. 3 (1973): 277-85; Voprosy sravnitel'noi pedagogiki, Moskovskii ped. institut im. V. I. Lenina, Uchenye zapiski, vol. 404 (1971).

12. See Mieczyslaw Pecherski, "Pojecie systema oswiatowowychowawczego, " Studia z pedagogiki porownawczej, pp. 30-43; Tadeusz Wiloch, Ustroj szkolny (Warsaw: Panstwowe Wydawnictwo Naukowe, 1973).

13. See Nigel Grant, Society, Schools, and Progress in Eastern Europe (Oxford: Pergamon Press, 1969); O. Anweiler, ed. , Bildungsreformen in Osteuropa (Stuttgart: Kohlhammer, 1969); Janina Langneau-Markiewicz, in Access to Education, ed. Alfred Sauvy (Plan Europe 3000, Project 1, vol. 3) (The Hague: Martinus Nijhoff, 1973), pp. 16-51, 108-20.

14. Such an approach to the problem of polytechnical education has been applied independently by two authors (in "East" and "West"), namely: Ignacy Szaniawski, Humanizacja pracy a funkcja a spoleczna szkoly (2nd ed. ; Warsaw: Ksiazka i wiedza, 1967); Gerlind Schmidt, Die polytechnische Bildung in der Sowjetunion und in der DDR, Didaktische Konzeptionen und Lösungsversuche (Erziehungswissenschaftliche

Veroffentlichungen des Osteuropa-Instituts an der Freien Universitat
Berlin, ed. Oskar Anweiler and Siegfried Baske, vol. 8) (Heidelberg:
Quelle und Meyer, 1973).

15. See A. M. Arsen'ev and F. F. Korol'ev, "Metodologicheskie
problemy sotsialisticheskoi pedagogiki," Problemy sotsialisticheskoi
pedagogiki (Moscow: Pedagogika, 1973), pp. 11-53; Helmut Konig,
"Probleme der Einheit des Logischen und Historischen in der Padagogik,"
Deutsche Zeitschrift fur Philosophie 21, no. 11 (1973): 1273-86.

16. Such as Jaan Pennar, Ivan I. Bakalo, and George Z. F. Bereday,
Modernization and Diversity in Soviet Education (New York: Praeger
Publishers, 1971).

17. See Robert C. Tucker, "Culture, Political Culture, and Communist Society," Political Science Quarterly 88, no. 2 (1973): 173-90.

18. For a detailed treatment of the problem, see Detlef Glowka,
"Konvergenztheorie und vergleichende Bildungsforschung," Bildung und
Erziehung 24, no. 6 (1971): 531-40.

19. Ursula Springer, "Problems in Comparative Curriculum
Research," Padagogische Forschung und padagogischer Fortschritt, ed.
Wolfgang Hilligen and Rudolf Raasch (Bielefeld: Bertelsmann, 1970),
pp. 139-52. Oskar Anweiler, "Curriculum Research from the Perspective
of Comparative Education," in Relevant Methods in Comparative Education, pp. 187-98.

20. An indication of the importance attached to the problem is the
topic of the second conference of educationists of socialist countries,
held in Berlin, August 12-16, 1974: "The education of all-round developed socialist personalities—the task of the national educational
systems in the socialist countries."

**YOUNG PEOPLE'S CHOICE
OF CAREERS AND MANPOWER
PLANNING IN THE SOVIET UNION**
Elisabeth Koutaissoff

Using a somewhat crude but convenient simplification, education
can be approached from either a producer's or a consumer's point of
view. For the producer, manpower is a factor of production and education a means to train an adequate work force. For the consumer, the
child or his parent, it is an opportunity to develop the physical and
mental potential of a human being. In a society where education is no
longer the mere transmission of an existing store of knowledge, skills,
and accepted values, the aims of education inevitably become a matter
of controversy. Any modern economy, whether planned or otherwise,
must make provisions for the upbringing of its child population and for
importing the country's prospective labor force the skills and knowledge
needed to run its industries, transport systems, hospitals, schools,
and administrative offices. Inevitably, statisticians and economists
are called in to calculate the prospective school population and the
number and qualifications of the teachers, then to work out the needs
of the labor market in respect of numbers and skills required, the costs
of education, and the return on investment in human capital.

Education seen as manpower training is very much within the Soviet
tradition, but it is apparent also in the recommendation of the U.S.
National Advisory Council on Vocational Training to the effect that "no
one ought to leave the educational system without a saleable skill,"[1]
and this aspect also was emphasized at the thirty-fourth International
Conference on Education organized by UNESCO in September 1973 in
Geneva under the heading, "The Relationship Between Education, Training, and Employment."

On the other hand, there is growing pressure from the consumers
of education (and from progressive educationists) to promote the free
development of the child's personality and to remove the constraints
that may impede the spontaneous manifestation of the creative potenti-
alities of the young. Hence the clamor to do away with l' ecole prison
and even for a "deschooling of society." Without going that far, one

participant at the 1973 Geneva Conference on Education attributed the
revolt of the young, to some extent at least, to government tendencies
to treat human beings as mere factors of production. [2]

Although there are obviously considerable discrepancies between
the aspirations of individuals and the requirements of society, they
need not necessarily be incompatible—provided the right balance is
struck between the demands of society and the willingness of individuals
to accept them.

In the USSR, manpower planning is an integral part of the overall
economic plan; consequently, education is geared to the needs of the
state rather than to the wishes of individuals. Yet career aspirations
of the young have become sufficiently explicit since the late 1950s to
warrant specialized sociological studies designed to assess and to
bridge the gap between the career aspirations of school leavers and
planned manpower requirements.

CAREER ASPIRATIONS OF SCHOOL LEAVERS

The earliest studies of school leavers' career aspirations were
carried out by the Novosibirsk University in conjunction with the Institute of Economics and Organization of Industrial Production in Siberia
in 1961, followed by the University of the Urals in Sverdlovsk. Sample
studies of a similar kind were later effected in the province of Leningrad
and the city itself, in Central Asian and Baltic Union Republics, and
in the Buriat Autonomous Soviet Socialist Republic (ASSR). [3] The investigations, by means of questionnaires and interviews, were conducted
among school leavers completing the eight-year school (aged 15 to 16)
and those completing the ten-year secondary school (aged 17 to 18).
Follow-up studies allowed correlation of the wishes expressed with
their realization one or several years later.

Questionnaires were of several types. Some merely asked respondents to estimate the attractiveness of professions according to a ten-
point scale or by ranking them. Others asked respondents to make a
personal choice from a long list comprising manual work professions
(such as miner, carpenter, turner) and intellectual ones (such as phi-
losopher, scientist, specialist in cybernetics). Some questionnaires
were designed to elucidate why a given profession was regarded as
desirable or otherwise; at what age it was first envisaged; who influenced the choice—parents, teachers, friends, or mass media (newspapers, radio, or TV). Other questionnaires were still more searching
and inquired about the respondent's school performance, use of free
time, wish to stay or change place of residence, parents' occupation,
family income, housing conditions (in square meters of floor space),
and the number of siblings in the family.

Information was collected over several years and in many localities
to ascertain the stability of preferences for definite professions and the

differences between juveniles of different nationalities and those living
in urban or rural areas. By the end of a decade it was becoming clear
that young people ranked intellectual professions much higher than
manual ones. The most coveted occupations were those of radio engi-
neer, pilot, mathematician, and physicist, while those of agricultural
worker, bookkeeper, shop assistant, waiter, cook, and house painter
came at the bottom of the list. Boys favored professions with a high
component of physics and mathematics, while girls preferred arts and
biology; so if their wishes were to be realized, all engineers would be
male while teachers and doctors would be female. Rural youths were
less averse to manual work and more realistic in their ambitions. Country girls ranked dressmaking and nursery school work higher than their
urban contemporaries. Leningrad school leavers set their targets high—
they wished to join the scientific staffs of research institutes, and
apparently often succeeded; at any rate, even quite responsible posts
in the Leningrad industries are filled by engineers born outside the
city. [4]

If one were to construct a graph showing the needs of the economy,
it would have the shape of a pyramid with a large base of agricultural
and industrial workers as well as service personnel, narrowing toward
an apex of highly qualified scientists and astronauts, while the wishes
of young people would be represented by a reverse pyramid with a tiny
base of those who (usually in rural areas) are prepared to accept heavy
manual work, broadening to a vast summit of specialists. [5] This term
is applied rather loosely in the USSR to white-collar workers with higher
or secondary specialized education (whose functions and standing in
the economy vary greatly), a group made even more heterogenous by the
inclusion of praktiki—men in senior positions in industry or public life
who have considerable practical experience but little formal education.
However, it is now customary to exclude from the class of specialists
persons engaged in nonmanual routine work such as bookkeepers, office clerks, typists, shop assistants, nursery school or junior medical
personnel, and other "employees" (sluzhashchie).

With social stratification largely based on educational achievement, up to 80 percent of all secondary school leavers try to enroll in
establishments of higher or secondary specialized education, but the
country lacks the material means to provide advanced education for all
and its economy cannot function without an adequate supply of manual
workers. Consequently, plans for employment and training are determined by the realities of present-day Soviet conditions.

MANPOWER PLANNING

Like most planning, this starts with the drawing up of "balances,"
estimating on the one hand the needs of the national economy, including the nonproductive sphere, and on the other, the availability of

human resources. Naturally, the quality as well as the size of the
work force has to be estimated; in other words, plans have to be drawn
up regarding the numbers and qualifications of specialists and skilled
workers as well as unskilled labor inputs. For a long time, forecasting
requirements in specialists was in the forefront because they had to be
balanced against the training facilities available in institutions of
higher and secondary specialized education. However, with a shrinking number of juveniles joining the labor force since the late 1950s,
the whole problem of manpower resources, their more rational use, and
the minimum educational standards to be achieved by the rank and file,
have become major concerns.

Specialists and Their Training

The techniques used in forecasting the needs in specialists are
still rather empirical. The initial step is to establish a fairly detailed
list of prospective job vacancies stating the qualifications required
from those who will fill them. In the case of existing enterprises, requests for additional staff sent by the enterprises are used, but such
requests are not always reliable because they tend to be inflated or
else unimaginative in the sense of failing to take account of changed
demands made on personnel resulting from changes in modes of production or the introduction of new products. However, they are useful for
estimating probable rates of attrition due to death, disablement, or
retirement (on average, 3 to 4 percent) and the number of praktiki to be
replaced by qualified specialists. The forecasting of personnel needs
for new enterprises is particularly troublesome; so are forecasts for
old plants that are being modernized, enlarged, or retooled, or where
new techniques and technologies are introduced, sometimes at short
notice as in 1958, when the importance of the chemical industry in
general and of plastics in particular created a demand for chemists.
Similarly, the recognition of the importance of economics and managerial skills has called for more specialists in these fields than had been
anticipated in the early 1960s.

In the case of long-term projects, when detailed lists are difficult
to compile, one resorts to the old "saturation" method, based on the
ratio of specialists per 100 workers most appropriate for a given industry, bearing in mind that such industries as engineering, electronics,
and radio technology require a higher percentage of specialists than,
say, the timber and textile industries. Furthermore, new scientific
discoveries lead to expanding research and development programs,
which in turn call for still more specialists.

As a result, during 1961-68, while investment in industry increased
at an annual average rate of 6.8 percent, the number of specialists rose
by 9.3 percent; for transport and communications, the respective in-

creases averaged 6. 3 percent for investment and 8. 7 percent for specialists. Only in the long neglected field of agriculture, where the ratio of specialists per 100 workers is already four times less than in industry, an 11 percent increase in investment brought about only a 7. 1 percent rise in the number of specialists employed. This is mainly due to their mass exodus from the countryside; indeed, out of 1. 1 million specialists trained during the 1958-68 decade, only about 155, 000 actually took up permanent jobs on collective and state farms while the remaining 85 percent found employment in other fields, usually unrelated to their training. [6]

The productive capacity of an enterprise, the complexity of the articles manufactured, and also the type of production (mass production or batch or single-model production) also are used as yardsticks to estimate needs in qualified personnel. Recently there has been a growing demand for experts in management, and it is hoped that this may lead to a streamlining of the often inflated administrative staffs, which account for 7 percent of the total industrial labor force (even 14 percent according to a letter to the editor in Literaturnaia gazeta, May 8, 1974). Moreover, since specialists are not always employed rationally and purposefully, a reduction in their numbers need not necessarily reduce the efficiency of a plant.

The wasteful use of highly qualified manpower is largely due to shortages of ancillary personnel, itself the outcome of ill-conceived savings on administrative staff and the low pay scales of "employees" as compared to those of skilled workers.

Manpower planning for the nonproductive sphere presents less difficulty as it is less directly affected by technological progress than the productive sphere. Estimates are mainly based on workloads such as the expected number of school children per class, the number of teaching hours per teacher, the number of hospital beds and the types of patients as they affect the work of doctors and nurses, the number of library users per library. Targets are set either to expand or improve facilities, and the major constraints are those imposed by state budget allocations. There are often competing claims: For example, should priority be given to train more (or more knowledgeable) nurses or to train swimming, skiing, or football teams for the Olympic games?

Although scientific progress may affect the nonproductive sphere less dramatically, it introduces new equipment into hospitals as well as into school and university laboratories. This in turn requires new types of medical specialists or teachers. Eventually, the crucial item for any further planning involves science and scientific cadres for research institutions, which are major claimants to the most highly qualified labor force. Indeed, while the total Soviet labor force approximately doubled between 1940 and 1970, specialists increased sevenfold and specialists employed in research institutes and design bureaus grew ninefold. [7]

Specialists are trained at establishments of higher education (vysshie uchebnye zavedeniia or VUZy) of which there were 825 in 1972, or at secondary specialized schools (srednie spetsial 'nye uchebnye zavedeniia or SSUZy) which numbered 4,270. The length of courses at VUZy averages five years despite measures taken to shorten them. That of SSUZ courses is usually two years for entrants with secondary education and four in the case of school leavers coming from the eight-year schools. During the period 1961-70, some 4,745,000 men and women graduated from VUZy and another 7 million completed SSUZ courses. According to plans put forward at the Twenty-fourth Party Congress, another 9 million specialists should graduate from VUZy and SSUZy in the course of the present five-year plan (1971-75). This would bring the overall number of specialists to 23 million by 1975, or approximately 20 percent of the total labor force.

The major centers of advanced courses in pure sciences and the humanities are the universities, which now number 63, the latest (1974) addition being the university of Nukus in Uzbekistan. [8] Among the more vocationally oriented VUZy in 1970 there were 230 engineering, 98 agricultural, 82 medical, and 198 pedagogical institutes as well as military, naval, music, art, and drama, and also higher Party schools. SSUZy also specialize in a variety of subjects; most are of the technicum type, but others train nurses and auxiliary medical personnel; teachers for junior forms and nursery schools; art, music, and physical educationists; as well as for other occupations including dentistry.

Apart from full-time day courses, most VUZy (and some SSUZy) have special departments of evening and correspondence courses. The latter are so important that 27 institutions are solely concerned with this type of course. A decree dated August 20, 1969, enjoined all VUZy to organize preparatory classes to enable young workers, peasants, and demobilized soldiers to prepare for VUZ entrance examinations and thus equalize their chances of admission with those of their more privileged competitors coming from better staffed and better equipped urban schools attended largely by children of better paid white-collar workers. These preparatory classes, which numbered 498 by 1970-71, are reminiscent of the earlier "workers' faculties" or rabfak (rabochie fakul'tety) and are designed to combat the emergence of a hereditary educationally superior elite, which is contrary to the policy of equal opportunity for all, now increasingly jeopardized by the hardening stratification of Soviet society. It is planned to have 20 percent of all VUZ entrants recruited from these preparatory courses, which is a far smaller figure than the 80 percent envisaged by the Khrushchev educational reforms.

The relative merits of full- and part-time study have been the subject of much controversy and many reforms and counterreforms. At present, full-time study has been accepted as the more efficient although more expensive form, a major expense being students' grants, which, however inadequate, absorb 27 to 28 percent of the total outlay of VUZy. (Staff salaries are, as usual, the largest item and account for 47 to 48 percent of state allocations to VUZy.) Furthermore, full-time students forgo earnings or, putting it otherwise, the loss of their labor is a loss to the national economy. Estimates made in 1968-69, showed that on average the training of a specialist costs the state 6,530 rubles, to which another 3,500 rubles are contributed by the family in maintenance, clothing, and so on. On the other hand, the state's outlay on the training of a specialist at extension courses amounted to about half that of a full-time student, while the labor contributed by a part-time student to the national economy exceeded the cost of his training, despite the cost to his enterprise of the time off he was entitled to take for exams and study.[9] However, these economic advantages are offset by educational disadvantages such as the high rate of failure (up to 50 percent of initial enrollment); lower standards of attainment; and shorter period of service after training—this averages 35 years of working life in the case of full-time students and 24 years in the case of extension students.[10] Furthermore, students who fail, withdraw, or change courses upset the planned output of VUZy and SSUZy and, consequently, the planned expansion of the specialist work force.

Admittedly, part-time study has been beneficial in the past and helped praktiki to raise their theoretical knowledge; in particular, in the postwar period extension courses enabled primary school teachers to qualify as subject teachers when rural four-year schools were converted first into seven-year schools (1949-50) and later into eight-year schools (1958-59). Even today, 60 percent of all correspondence course students are teachers.[11] More recently, part-time courses have been organized in the economics of production, statistics, accounting, and allied subjects for senior managerial personnel, engineers, technicians, and collective farm (kolkhoz) chairmen in connection with the drive for an understanding of economic factors by the population at large, a drive culminating in the foundation in 1971 of the Moscow Institute of Planning and Management for top managerial personnel including heads of industrial ministries.

A major feature of present-day Soviet education is a search for ways of raising standards: (1) by means of various refresher courses designed periodically to upgrade and update standards (to be discussed further with special reference to the teaching profession) and (2) by associating VUZy with appropriate scientific-research institutes (nauchnoissledovatel'skie instituty or NII), or with particularly modern, well-equipped industrial enterprises, or both, the latter being the most novel trend.

To appreciate the significance of such associations, one should recall that from the time of the Russian Revolution and well into the 1950s, universities and other establishments of higher education were merely mass teaching institutions where no research work was carried on. The latter was concentrated in the scientific research institutes (NII) of the Academy of Sciences of the USSR, the medical and the agricultural academies, the academies of sciences of the Union Republics, and the institutes subordinate to various ministries. Only the most famous universities—like those of Moscow, Leningrad, and some other

towns—and the most renowned technical schools like the Moscow Bauman Polytechnicum, had distinguished scientists and scholars on their
staffs. Other VUZy, especially pedagogical institutes, were staffed
by men and women who seldom ventured beyond the established programs and whose knowledge hardly exceeded that of the textbooks used.
    Collaboration and in some cases the integration of VUZ and NII is
a relatively new phenomenon and can be roughly dated from 1957, when
the newly founded and now famous Novosibirsk branch of the Academy
of Sciences established close contacts with the University of Novosibirsk. The merging of certain higher technical institutes (vysshie
tekhnicheskie uchebnye zavedeniia or VTUZy) with major industrial
plants began in response to Khrushchev's insistence on the practical
aspects of education. Among these zavod-VTUZy, the best known is
the one based on the Likhachev automobile works in Moscow. About
the same time, VUZy were encouraged to undertake research for individual plants and, as from 1966, to retain up to 75 percent of the
balances between the sums paid by industry and their actual expendi-
tures on research. This arrangement benefited VUZy financially, particularly since VUZy do not receive any allocations for research work
from the state budget. Lately, these contracts between VUZy and individual plants have come under criticism as detracting VUZ scientists
from fundamental research and channeling their efforts toward narrowly
specialized practical issues. On the contrary, association with appropriate NII involves VUZ staffs and senior students in the process of
truly scientific research. Involvement in research work is beneficial
for senior students both as a teaching device and as a method of selecting those capable of original work, who then proceed through
aspirantura to the higher degrees of candidate and doctor of science.
    Aspiranty formerly were trained solely at NII, but now a growing
number of VUZy (including pedagogical institutes) have secured the
privilege of training research students. This is a mixed blessing. On
the one hand, NII can train only about 25 percent of the postgraduates
required by the growing needs of the sceintific and technical revolution;
on the other, some VUZy have neither the staff nor the equipment for
serious research work. [12] To forestall a deterioration of standards, all
higher degrees have to be confirmed by a special commission known as
VAK (vysshaia attetatsionnaia komissiia) of the Ministry of Higher and
Secondary Specialized Education of the USSR. Doctorates are awarded
either on the merit of published work or on the submission of a thesis.
Considerable controversy has arisen lately over the efficiency of this
double tier of degree awards (that is, those of candidate and doctor),
the standards of dissertations submitted, and the composition of VAK.
The latter comprises permanent members who may not be competent to
judge the very specialized topic of a thesis that is only marginally related to their own field. Moreover, some members of VAK are appointees
of a previous era (according to Zhores Medvedev, Lysenko is still a
member of VAK). The importance of a vaild system of certification is
twofold: (1) research institutes recruit their staffs on the basis of

degrees, so discernment in assessing the scientific potential of applicants is bound to affect Soviet science as such; (2) salaries and pro-
motions are related to degrees, and the latter may be coveted for
personal careers rather than the promotion of knowledge. *

Apart from collaboration between VUZy and industrial plants, and
that of VUZ and NII, a more recent trend is to achieve integration of
teaching, research, and production. Collaboration between a few NII
and industrial plants started in response to the difficulties experienced
by research institutions in getting their inventions and innovations introduced into actual production. Only about 30 to 35 percent of all
improvements that had successfully undergone laboratory tests were
taken over by industry, sometimes with delays that made them obso-
lescent. Associations of NII and industrial plants started in 1968 and
were stepped up in 1971 after the Twenty-fourth Party Congress. For
example, an association was formed by the Leningrad Technological
Institute with the Lengiprokhim NII (and its branches in Chimkent and
Togliatti) and the Nevsky chemical works. It is hoped to draw in
Gosplan and institutes of economics. Associations could be either of
a local type involving only specific branches of production, or they
might be of All-Union importance and headed by major scientific institutions with appropriate feedback and mutual enrichment.

Apart from the obvious advantages of such associations where
ideas could be generated, experimentally tested, and disseminated via
newly designed courses for students, VUZy would have access to better
and newer equipment. Hitherto equipment was a real problem for VUZy,
partly because allocations to new or expanding VUZy are still based on
estimates made in the 1950s of the "chalk and blackboard" type (that
is, before the advent of such costly hardware as computers, electron
microscopes, and language laboratories) and partly because the Ministry of Higher and Secondary Specialized Education has only one
specialized design bureau (with a branch in Odessa) that both designs
and manufactures equipment requested by VUZy. Often these requests
are not met because the equipment is not being manufactured yet or has
not even been designed. So VUZy resort to making it in their own

---

*In its issue of May 15, 1974, Literaturnaia gazeta launched a
questionnaire on the usefulness and composition of VAK, to be answered
by readers who were scientific workers. The questionnaire was drafted
in consultation with the Institute of History of Natural Science and
Technology of the Academy of Sciences of the USSR. Preliminary results
published on July 10 showed that over 3,700 respondents or 62.8 percent (69.1 percent of doctorate holders) favored a periodic renovation
of VAK membership carried out in consultation with leading experts.
There was greater divergence on methods of fixing the pay scales of
scientific workers, preference (32.4 percent) going to a scheme that
would guarantee a basic minimum to be supplemented by payments for
work done.

workshops, which is neither economical nor efficient. Difficulties in obtaining new equipment or replacing old models, which are made to last nine to ten years instead of two to three, are exacerbated by delays in actual construction of new or extensions to old VUZy. This means either curtailing the intake of students or suffering from overcrowding. Delays of up to ten years have occurred, as on the new site of the Bauman Polytechnical Institute, because the ministries responsible for building materials, construction, and installation of heating, lighting, telephone, and laboratory equipment are themselves handicapped by inadequate material facilities. [13]

Whatever the outcome of plans for such research-teaching-production associations, [14] the major present concern is no longer the training on a mass scale of maintenance engineers, physicians for rural outpatient departments, and rank-and-file teachers, but a search for talent and for giving it the best possible opportunities to do original and creative work. Exceptionally gifted men are needed to promote scientific progress and also to set up new faculties and departments today to train the scientists of tomorrow who will become fully "operative" in five to fifteen years' time, perhaps even by the year 2000. In a sense, planning becomes futurology.

Nonspecialist Education and Employment

Until the late 1950s, the recruitment of unskilled labor presented no problem. Information on the number of school leavers available for employment was known from school statistics. Newcomers required for semiskilled work usually learned it by on-the-job training, occasionally at factory schools (fabrichno-zavodskoe obuchenie or FZO) attached to larger factories, while some came from state labor reserve schools. Rural youths, unless recruited to labor reserve schools or directly by industry and construction (or called up for military service), remained on the farms.

However, heavy war losses in the most fertile age groups and the less explicable fall in the birth rate since 1960 are causing a shortage of juvenile labor. This first became manifest in 1959-62, when the number of young workers entering the labor force fell below that of people retiring from it. These were the depleted cohorts born during the war years. The position improved slightly later in the 1960s but is expected to deteriorate again from 1975, when the impact of the falling birth rate will begin to tell.

To compensate for the shrinking number of juveniles, Soviet planners took various steps to draw in people still employed in their homes and on their land plots. As a result, between the 1959 and 1970 censuses the number of these people decreased from 17.9 to 5.9 million. One way of achieving this was to site new industries not in the traditional manner (nearest to sources of raw materials or energy or to transport facilities) but in small and medium-sized towns where there were people, mainly married women immobilized by family duties, who could be drawn in if jobs were, so to speak, brought to their doorsteps. This supply of labor is now exhausted in the Russian Soviet Federated Socialist Republic (RSFSR), Ukraine, Latvia, and Estonia, although not yet in the rural overpopulated areas of the Central Asian republics, Transcaucasia, Moldavia, and the Northern Caucasus (and to a lesser extent in the westernmost districts of Belorussia and Ukraine), where the birthrate is still high.

So, whereas in the planning of specialist manpower the main constraint is the capacity of VUZy and SSUZy to train adequate numbers and types of specialists, in the planning of less skilled manpower, the demographic factor takes on overriding importance. The demand for a better-educated labor force (that is, for longer schooling) further reduces the number of juveniles entering employment, although this is a delay rather than a reduction. Lastly, a new factor has to be taken into account, namely, the personal wishes of the young, who have now gained a certain "scarcity value."

Strictly speaking the labor shortage is not acute, but it is a new problem in the USSR. It probably could be overcome by a better deployment of manpower, greater mechanization, and changed attitudes to certain occupations among the young. A survey of the professional composition of workers carried out in 1969 revealed that over half the work force in industry and 60 percent in construction was doing manual work. [15] The proportion of the latter is even greater in agriculture, yet the belated endeavors to increase mechanization in agriculture are handicapped, paradoxically, in both the most underpopulated and the most overpopulated regions. In northern and central Russia, with decreasing population, machinery can be used at best by one shift and occasionally not at all because the young have left and the remaining aging and mostly female population is incapable of learning how to handle complex mechanisms or physically unfit to do so. As a result, between 1940 and 1966 some 7.8 million hectares (ha) of agricultural land, of which 4.8 million were arable, have ceased to be cultivated in the non-black earth zone of the RSFSR, and another 2 million ha (24 percent of the total) in the Baltic republics. [16] (One hectare equals 2.47 acres.) Contrariwise, in the overpopulated southern Union Republics, machinery cannot be fully used either, because this would deprive collective farmers of labor-day earnings, and consequently infringe on their right to work, guaranteed by the Constitution. [17]

The wasteful use of manpower and the persistence of manual work can be blamed on both inadequate mechanization and the low level of education of a fairly large minority consisting mainly of older people but also including 13 million men and women aged 30 to 39 who never got beyond the fourth grade. [18]

The situation has some similarities with that of foreign workers in the industrialized countries of Western Europe who have been essential to Europe's industries although most are unskilled and some even illiterate in their own languages. According to a survey by W. R. Bohning, "the potential for the employment of foreigners in the manufacturing and post-industrial societies is far from exhausted and even may become greater as new technology is introduced," because the latter may require high-frequency repetitive jobs and shift work and, in the past, "employers often adapted their pattern of demand to the type of labor available, i. e., to the foreigner with unknown skills and little understanding of the host language."[19]

The level of education needed by workers in an industrial society has been the subject of considerable debate in the USSR. The expansion of secondary education confronts Soviet managers with educated yet unskilled young workers. These teenagers are at a disadvantage when compared to their former classmates who, having left school two years earlier, have meanwhile learned a trade either by attending vocational schools or, more commonly, by on-the-job training. The problem of program content for teenagers over 15 is not peculiar to the Soviet Union but to all industrialized countries whose educational systems are in search of new forms of secondary education, since the latter is no longer designed to cater to an elite but open to all adolescents and should provide a broad general education yet prepare for some definite occupation. Everywhere the fundamental trouble is a lack of synchronization between rising educational standards and the slow expansion of opportunities for creative, interesting forms of work. Even the manufacture of highly sophisticated articles is often carried out by the old soul-destroying conveyor belt methods. These are likely to persist until the time when fully automated production lines come universally into existence. Meanwhile, there is distinct disappointment and dissatisfaction among young people with monotonous, repetitive work. The outward manifestation of job dissatisfaction is a high labor turnover, which is damaging to the economy and to the individual as well. It has been estimated that the time spent by a worker to find a new job averages 33 days, and for young people under twenty the period of unemployment may average 41 days or more.[20] Any skills learned by on-the-job training are a dead loss for the factory, which has used skilled workers' time to instruct the teenagers and also has borne the costs arising from the inability of apprentices to fulfill the average norms and their tendency to damage tools and produce rejects.

Juveniles under 18 years of age are entitled to shorter hours at specified apprentice rates of remuneration. On completing their training, they are transferred to normal rates of pay. However, lack of experience and dexterity often preclude their fulfilling adult norms and, consequently, earning a full day's pay. It therefore pays them to start over as apprentices in some other occupation. The costs of their retraining (usually amounting to 250 to 350 rubles per trainee) fall on the

new employer, which means in effect the Soviet state. Apart from economic losses, job flitting engenders restlessness, while disappointment with a career may have an adverse and even traumatic effect on
morale. [21]

Juvenile labor turnover has been investigated by various sociologists. Surveys made in the early 1960s tended to show that teenagers
who had not progressed beyond the eighth grade adapted better to industrial work, were less impatient with dull, repetitive jobs, and less
liable to become job flitters than secondary school leavers. These conclusions have been challenged since on the grounds that, when the
earlier labor turnover surveys were carried out, most secondary school
leavers in industry were there just to gain the two years' productive
work qualification demanded from VUZ entrants under the 1958 (Khrushchev) regulations. According to more recent studies, better-educated
youngsters become better workers because they learn new skills more
quickly and rise faster from one level of skill to the next (razriad). [22]
The position could then be summed up approximately by saying that the
less educated young workers adapt better under present conditions but
the more educated will adapt better to technological change and learn
trades that do not exist today.

The latter point of view has now prevailed in the USSR, and all
eight-year schools are to become ten-year schools, while vocational
schools will be gradually converted into institutions providing both
vocational training and full secondary education. Like Khrushchev's
reforms aimed at introducing productive work into general education
schools, the upgrading of vocational schools seeks to combine academic study with practical know-how, but in a sense it starts at the
other end. The earlier scheme floundered on the inadequacy of the
material facilities made available to schools, with the result that pupils learned to handle outdated machinery or specialized in a single
simple trade like bread making, sewing, or woodwork. The present
scheme may flounder on a shortage of teachers. But it should be wel-
comed as an attempt to raise a generation of educated workers and also
remove a long-standing social injustice occasioned by the low status
of vocational schools, which even administratively come not under
any ministry of education but under a special committee for professional
and technical education of the Council of Ministers of the USSR.

Upgrading Vocational Schools

The forerunners of these vocational schools (professional'notekh-
nicheskie uchilishcha or PTU) were the labor reserve schools, organized in 1940, offering six-month to two-year courses to train
peasant boys and girls with a four-year education and urban teenagers
with seven years' schooling for the simplest manual occupations. At
first enrollment was by compulsory drafting based on the size of population of a village or industrial settlement. Later enrollment became

voluntary and standards improved with the extension of seven years'
schooling to rural areas and later still the introduction of the universal
eight-year school. Pupils who completed the course were liable to be
assigned to specific jobs for four years, an obligation that compared
unfavorably with the three-year assignments of VUZ and SSUZ graduates
who had benefited by a longer education at state expense (and this still
is the case in respect of PTU pupils). No opportunities existed for
youngsters coming from labor reserve schools to reenter the general
education stream apart from evening and correspondence courses, and
the position is not much better for PTU pupils. In 1974, there were
5,900 PTU catering for 2.8 million pupils. Some PTU, particularly the
railway schools with their two-year course, were popular from the out-
set, but on the whole PTU were mainly attended by school dropouts,
children of single women, pensioners, poorly paid workers, and, generally speaking, boys (rather than girls) anxious to enter paid employment as early as possible. Actual enrollment often fell below plan.

The upgrading of PTU into institutions providing secondary education, begun in 1969-70, will change their status completely since their
pupils will be able to sit for VUZ entrance examinations pari passu
with other secondary school leavers, while from the point of view of
immediate employment they will have an advantage over their contemporaries coming up from general education schools. However, conversion will be gradual for the adjustments to be made are very great. To
begin with, the length of the course will be increased from the present
one, two, or (very occasionally) three years to a full four. The syllabus
will have to be revised. At present, practical work in PTU takes up 60
to 65 percent of school hours and much of it is devoted to the acquisition of menial craft skills closely geared to the 1,100 to 1,200 occupations for which PTU train their pupils. Henceforth instruction is to
become broadly polytechnical and PTU will be grouped into five main
types, those oriented toward: (1) chemistry and metallurgy, (2) radio
and electrotechnology, (3) metal working, (4) mechanics and assembly,
and (5) biology and agricultural sciences. A new course in the economics of labor and production is to be introduced and greater emphasis
will be put on "social sciences." The actual buildings will have to be
improved and reequipped.

A major difficulty in the conversion of PTU into secondary schools
is likely to be a shortage of teachers, especially of suitably trained
teachers of labor subjects. Hitherto these were taught by mastera
(foremen or skilled workers), very few of whom had much formal education while even fewer had attended courses in didactics or methods of
teaching. Special industrial-pedagogical faculties at nine pedagogical
institutes were started only recently. At 30 to 40 others there are departments providing combined courses in physics (or chemistry or biology) and general technical disciplines as well as 17 faculties of
fine and graphic arts with departments of artistic design and labor to
teach pupils entering the service industries. Most teachers of labor

specialize in either technical labor or the mechanization of agriculture. Only the Kiev Pedagogical Institute offers all three options—technical labor, mechanization of agriculture, and service industries—but its students are largely oriented toward work in schools for the handicapped. [23]

The special faculties are now supplemented by industrial-technological technicums of proftekhobrazovanie at SSUZ level. It is hoped that graduates of these institutions will be able to instill some reverence for industrial and agricultural work among their pupils, to participate in vocational guidance, and to act as career advisers.

The present general drive to raise the qualifications of specialists in all walks of life by sending them to refresher courses at major universities and polytechnicums, especially those connected with NII or progressive industrial enterprises, also extends to the teaching profession. Both secondary school teachers and lecturers at smaller provincial VUZy are being sent to vacation or longer courses organized by the appropriate faculties of universities and major pedagogical institutes. These courses are designed to modernize the teachers' and lecturers' knowledge of their special subject, to instruct them in the use of advanced educational technology, to broaden their understanding of psychology, and to raise the level of their involvement in communist education. For the latter purpose and in order to raise the standards of lecturers in social science, there are special institutes organized by major universities engaged in introducing the new courses in scientific communism. As to lecturers in education and didactics, their retraining is the responsibility of the Moscow Institute for Advanced Training of lecturers of pedagogical departments of universities and of pedagogical institutes.

Similarly, there are courses for the "improvement of teachers" (usovershenstvovanie uchitelei), which have been gathering momentum since the Second All-Union Congress of Teachers in July 1968. They are organized by the constituent institutes of the Academy of Educational Sciences, the NII of Education of Union Republics and leading pedagogical institutes, all of which have experimental schools attached to them (bazovye shkoly). By 1973, the number of establishments providing courses for raising teachers' standards had risen to 178 and it was hoped that all teachers would have the opportunity of attending refresher courses every five years. There were also ten faculties for raising the qualifications of heads of schools. [24]

This retraining is necessary partly because of the still inadequate qualifications of many teachers and partly because of the modernization of the curriculum and teaching methods that began in 1966 and is still in progress. Educationists are in search of new methods designed to introduce more theoretical knowledge in junior forms in an accessible way, to cut down on memory work, and to develop instead powers of reasoning, observation, and independent thought (razvivaiushchee obuchenie). Refresher courses also aim at diversifying teachers' interests and thus making them capable of introducing optional courses, some of which have a practical bent and facilitate vocational guidance.

Communist Education

Most aims and difficulties encountered by Soviet educationists are similar to those of their opposite numbers in the industrialized Western countries. There is, however, one feature that is characteristic solely of Soviet education. It is the ceaseless ideological and political indoctrination of youth. This has always existed but is becoming a pathologically obsessive concern. The subject is too vast to be treated even cursorily in a short essay, but it is such an important component of Soviet education that it has to be at least mentioned. The term political indoctrination is perhaps too narrow to describe communist education, which is a search for a new secular ethic and an attempt to form a "new man." It is all-pervasive and yet it has a variety of aspects: rational, emotional, and practical. It includes character formation, the internalization of political and moral convictions, esthetic appreciation, unswerving loyalty to the Party, and faith in the desirability and ineluctability of its goals, absence of doubt or criticism of the means to achieve these goals, patriotism (which does not exclude internationalism), a spirit of public service, and respect for the law in general and state property in particular—in fact, a mixture of a laudably humanistic code of behavior with an unquestioning acceptance of very questionable dogmatic assertions. The study of Marxism-Leninism, which has always been part of any VUZ course, is now supplemented by practical assignments. These range from addressing trade-union, school, and housing estate meetings on political topics to participation in unpaid vacation work on some remote construction site (labor semester). It is hoped that practical experience will foster in young specialists qualities of leadership and organizing abilities without detriment to the standards of their scientific competence.[25] One wonders whether some of the ideology now instilled into youth may not eventually come into conflict with mental attitudes resulting from razvivaiushchee obuchenie (habits of logical reasoning and scientific inquisitiveness), at least among some sectors of the population.

There are no signs yet of a conflict of generations except for a few undesirable trends such as contempt for manual work, widespread slothfulness, the acquisitive mentality of a consumer society, and, apparently, indifference toward the Party's loftier goals since such a persistent and concerted effort at indoctrination is demanded from members of the Party and Komsomol, from teachers, mass media, and parents.

The more general problem raised by P. L. Alston on the contradiction between school programs that reflect the outlook of an older generation, an outlook based on its life experience, and the aspirations of those who will live in a very different world in the days to come—this contradiction is probably less acute in the USSR where affluence is still something new and relative and, therefore, the aim of building the material and technical basis of communism is acceptable to both young and old, whereas in the West the ideal of the welfare state is taken for granted by the young and no longer appreciated as a great achievement. What is beginning to be questioned by Soviet youth is not so much the goal as the means that cause the depletion of natural resources, pollution, and the curtailment of human freedoms.

Vocational Guidance

Among the measures taken to overcome young people's reluctance to engage in manual occupations, particularly in agriculture and the service industries, is the prominence given to vocational guidance. If the latter is to help reconcile the interests of the economy and those of the individual, it must find ways to match aptitudes and demands made by work processes on the human organism. Of course, a preliminary step in vocational guidance is to know what jobs exist and to provide school leavers with much more detailed information regarding occupations, especially those suffering from a labor shortage not necessarily because they are exceptionally unpleasant but because of prejudice built up over the years; for example, "sitting in an office" is tantamount to desertion from hard, honorable toil, while being a salesman is regarded as equivalent to lining one's own pocket. Lack of adequate information often misleads even students into choosing the "wrong" faculty, with the result that they have to change courses or withdraw altogether. However, disseminating information about professions, glamorizing their attractiveness, or appealing to the public spirit of Soviet youth and creating a favorable climate for occupations that the country needs is, so to speak, "applied vocational guidance." More interesting are its theoretical aspects, namely, the work being done in the USSR on matching occupations and aptitudes.

THE STUDY OF OCCUPATIONS AND APTITUDES

The study of occupations starts with a breakdown of their various components, which are analyzed both theoretically and experimentally. In the theoretical approach, the objects of labor, the tools of production, the purposes to be achieved by each work process, and the knowledge and skill required to perform them are scrutinized in turn. The objects of labor usually are raw materials, semifinished goods, and energy, but not necessarily so. According to E. A. Klimov, head of Vocational Training, objects of labor can be living organisms, and not only cultivated plants but conditions that affect them such as soil, moisture, pests, and weeds—in fact, in agriculture, a whole set of

biological and physiochemical factors. The object of labor in service
industries is the customer and his social and psychological makeup.
Or it can be a system of signs, for instance, in type setting or punch-
card operations. So one can construct a table with the following five
columns: (1) man and nature (bionic professions), (2) man and machines
(technical professions), (3) man and man (socionomic), (4) man and
system of notation (signomic), and (5) man and artistic representation
(artonomic professions). Within each of these five groups one finds
occupations requiring vocational, secondary specialized, or higher
education. Thus, under man—nature, the less skilled occupations are
those of workers in agriculture or animal husbandry, market gardening,
and bee keeping; at secondary or VUZ levels, those of agronomist,
veterinary surgeon, or forester. In the man—man, column, at the lower
level are waiters, salesmen, and librarians of mass libraries; at the
secondary level, teachers in junior grades, nurses, nursery school
assistants, commercial technicians and organizers at VUZ level,
teachers, doctors, trade organizers, production engineers. Similarly,
signomic occupations range from type setter, shorthand typist, and
telephone operator to specialists in theoretical sciences.

Another way of classifying professions is according to the tools
and means of production. They can be broken down into four groups:
manual, mechanical, automated, and functional, the latter using the
functional properties of the human organism. Here, too, one finds
strange bedfellows. For instance, among people engaged in manual
work are carpenters, fitters, pianists, and surgeons. Among the
functionalists—teachers, actors, radio broadcasters, conductors, and
choirmasters.

A classification based on the purpose of work processes consists
of three groupings: gnostic (cognitive), transformatory, and research
activities. The purposes of the first group are to recognize, identify,
distinguish, and verify; those of the second are to transform, grind,
polish, influence, or service; and those of the last are to invent or
discover new results or models.

If one combines the first table (classification according to objects
of labor) with that of purposes, one finds in the first column (gnostic
occupations), controllers or agricultural production; under the second
(transformatory), workers in agriculture, animal husbandry, and forestry; and under the third (research), scientists engaged in plant and
animal breeding. By similarly combining the column man—artistic representation with the table of purposes, one finds under gnostic, super-
visors of house-painting and paper-hanging work; under transformatory,
house painters, engravers, sculptors, and jewelers; under research,
model designers, painters, composers, and writers.

Within this general framework are finer subdivisions. Thus, the
same object of labor may have different properties: for a fitter the
hardness of the metal is of major importance, whereas for the black-
smith it is its malleability at high temperature, and for the steel worker

its point of fusion or the presence of admixtures or other properties connected with smelting.[26]

Apart from such theoretical classifications, numerous practical work studies are being carried out on the lines of the "time and motion" evaluations used in norm setting, but with considerably more sophistication and taking more account of the worker's cognitive faculties. These studies are connected with the increasing interest in engineering psychology and ergonomics. The latter came to the fore in the late 1950s and the first conference on problems of engineering psychology was held in 1964, followed by a much larger conference on ergonomics in Moscow in the summer of 1972, which was attended by representatives of the Comecon countries and Yugoslavia. It brought together psychologists, physiologists, anthropologists, medical men, economists, designers, mathematicians, and sociologists.

Research is focused on the way work processes affect the human organism. Apart from external factors such as temperature, lighting, noise, and dust, every aspect of motion and expenditure of energy is measured, with minor motions like eye movement being recorded on film. Investigations bear on the speed of sensory and motor reactions required from the worker as well as changes in pulse rate, blood pressure, and rate of breathing that occur in the course of the work process. For instance, the effect of monotonous work on two groups of workers, one of which was more productive than the other, was measured by recording the frequency and energy of α-rhythm in the brain and psychogalvanic skin resistance at the beginning and end of the working day.[27] Types of recurrent errors also are subjected to analysis, and workers' own comments and evaluations are taken into account. Such detailed breakdowns of the demands made on the human organism allow one to establish professiograms or job profiles on the basis of which it becomes possible to forecast what aptitudes will be required from the worker for a definite job. Since the aim of these studies is also to better adapt the work place to the person, esthetic considerations are taken into account in the designing of new tools and machines. Indeed, one of the centers of ergonomics in the USSR is the All-Union NII of Technical Esthetics of the State Committee on Science and Technology of the Council of Ministers of the USSR.

There are, generally speaking, many tests and methods of evaluating such aptitudes as perception, memory, habit formation, and response to oncoming information, as well as for detecting physical defects like poor sight, hearing, or tactile discrimination, or character traits that may preclude success in certain occupations. However, the contrary approach, that of choosing the job for the individual rather than the individual for the job, is less common. Nor is there any consensus about whether or not there are specific gifts or abilities for ordinary semiskilled mass occupations. For K. M. Gurevich, head of the Laboratory of Psychophysical Problems of Professional Suitability of the NII of General and Educational Psychology of the Academy of

Educational Sciences, the main condition for success in such occupations is a "positive attitude to work," that is, motivation. He would
limit aptitude testing to occupations that present unforeseen and often
dangerous situations necessitating a great speed of reaction to an
overwhelming flow of information and neurological stability in stress
situations. [28] Others, however, think that one can at least determine
the physical and psychological inclinations that better fit a teenager
for certain occupations than others and will keep him reasonably happy
in his job. In any case, the Section of Pedagogy and Psychology of
Professional and Technical Training and Vocational Guidance is being
set up by the Academy of Educational Sciences on the basis of its NII
of Labor Education and Vocational Guidance. This will be the academy's
fourth section, the others being: Theory and History of Education, with
four NII; Didactics and Subject Teaching Methods, with five NII; and
Psychology and Developmental Physiology, with three NII. [29]

In the USSR, aptitude testing is closely linked to the measurement
of physiological factors. Intelligence tests are still frowned upon and
have not been used since the onslaught on pedology in the 1930s because performance in these tests measures achievement and thus reflects social and environmental factors as well as mental endowment,
to the disadvantage of children from deprived homes or areas. The
objection to aptitude tests had been that they are designed to select
or reject an individual for an occupation; in other words, they are an
employer's device, whereas aptitude tests in a socialist country should
help the individual to select his job. Therefore, aptitude tests should
be combined with a personal "professional consultation" (the word
"professional" being used in its Russian sense and relating to the teenager's prospective profession).

Most Soviet aptitude tests are designed to measure sensory perception and motor reactions to external stimuli: discrimination thresholds of visual images; sound pitch or roughness of surfaces; the speed
and precision of visual, auditory, and tactile reactions; digital dexterity; short-term visual memory; pulse and breathing rate changes in
response to sensory stimuli; the sense of time and spatial orientation;
auditory location. Some experiments in the recovery of bodily balance
seem to be a spinoff from astronaut training, but they are applicable
to circus artists performing on trapezes or building workers on high
constructions and power transmission pylons.

There is much interest in the connections of sense organs with
definite parts of the brain and the more elusive measurements by means
of encephalograms of the participation of certain areas of the cortex
in thought processes. A better understanding of the neurological basis
of temperament, and hence of behavior, is needed in the selection of
men for highly responsible jobs (such as those in charge of electrical
grid systems) who may have to contend with sudden emergencies when
the brain's powers of discrimination are severely taxed by the onrush
of information and the response of the nervous system must be rapid,

appropriate, and determined. At a conference on the psychophysiological bases of occupational selection held in Kiev in October 1973, the discussions centered on the basic properties of the nervous system, cortical and subcortical interaction, and the thresholds of sensitivity of sense organs necessary for learning common trades and professions. [30]

This preoccupation with the physiological aspect of aptitudes may be due to a Pavlovian tradition, or to the underlying materialistic philosophy, or to the fact that aptitude testing began as an offshoot of medical checkups in the army and in recruiting young workers for heavy industrial work, or because many of the studies are still carried out by medical men (at the Institute of Child and Adolescent Hygiene of the Ministry of Health of the USSR in Moscow, the Department of Medical Psychology and Psychiatry of the Voroshilovgrad Medical Institute, and elsewhere).

Although much of the research and many of the findings of specialists in the psychology of labor and in ergonomics are still confined within the walls of the respective NII and the pages of specialized periodicals, the search to adapt work to man rather than to allow him to remain "an appendage of the machine" has definitely started. Gosplan still computes its labor requirements in labor-power inputs and plans the training of human beings as investments for an expanding economy. Yet the human factors are slowly surfacing and beginning to exert a silent yet unrelenting pressure. Already there is talk of redesigning agricultural machinery to make it lighter and easier to handle by women, as well as providing lifting gear and transport on the kolkhoz.

In order to become self-sufficient in foodstuffs, the Soviet Union must and probably can—at a cost—make agricultural work attractive and lure people back to the villages where their parents toiled under inhuman conditions after collectivization. It will probably take even longer to transform industrial work into an inspiring and creative activity. More amenities for leisure time may act, as in the West, as acceptable temporary palliatives, although this does not solve the fundamental issue of work ceasing to be man's Old Testament curse and becoming the natural urge of homo factor. Alternatively, it has been suggested that, to make industrial work more meaningful to the individual and increase his personal involvement, there should be more effective worker participation in the management of the plant and even at higher echelons of decision making, [31] that the spirit of genuine emulation be revived in the now formalized and ossified systems of socialist competition, and that readier and more encouraging attention be given to the proposals of rationalizers, although they often do not amount to much.

It is too early to judge what the present research scientists will be able to achieve through ergonomics, vocational guidance, and mass persuasion, but it looks as if the real workers' revolution is getting under way.

NOTES

1. Quoted in Progress of Education in the United States of America:
1970-71 and 1971-72, U.S. Department of Health, Education, and Welfare Publication no. (OE) 73-19104, (Washington, D.C., 1973), p. 38.
2. Pierre Dominice, Young People's Attitudes to School, the Adult
World and Employment, Ed/BIE/34/Ref. 6, International Conference on
Education, 34th Session (Geneva, September 19-27, 1973), pp. 3-7.
3. According to V. N. Boriaz in Molodezh': metodologicheskie
problemy issledovaniia (Leningrad: Nauka, Leningradskoe otdelenie,
1973), pp. 31, 33, 35, no sociological studies of youth in general
were published between 1945 and 1953, whereas between 1953 and
1970 no fewer than 91 books and pamphlets dealt with the subject, as
well as 845 articles and 1,135 papers presented on various occasions.
Among studies concerned with school leavers' career aspirations are:
V. N. Shubkin, Sotsiologicheskie opyty (Moscow: Mysl', 1970), chapter 4; M. N. Rutkevich and F. R. Filippov, Sotsial 'nye peremeshcheniia
(Moscow: Mysl', 1970), chapter 6; E. K. Vasil'eva, Sotsial'no-
professional'nyi uroven' gorodskoi molodezhi (Leningrad: Izdatel' stvo
Leningradskogo universiteta, 1973), esp. pp. 35-36. An account of
the earlier studies is available in English in Murray Yanowitch and
Norton T. Dodge, "The Social Evaluation of Occupations in the Soviet
Union," Slavic Review 28, no. 4 (1969): 619-43.
4. Vasil'eva, Sotsial'no-professional'nyi uroven', pp. 91, 126.
5. Shubkin, Sotsiologicheskie opyty, p. 208.
6. V. E. Komarov, Ekonomicheskie problemy podgotovki i ispol'
zovaniia kadrov spetsialistov (Moscow: Ekonomike, 1972), pp. 42ff.
Mervyn Matthews, Class and Society in Soviet Russia (London: Allan
Lane—The Penguin Press, 1972), p. 342, calculates that although
361,000 persons between 1958 and 1968 "took degrees in agriculture
and forestry, yet the number of specialists employed in these branches
of the economy rose by only 115,000 from 130,000 to 246,000. Retirement would have accounted for 30,000 at most, so about two-thirds of
the newcomers must have deserted over the period." The discrepancy
in the figures quoted by Komarov and Matthews may be due to the former having included and the latter having excluded specialists with
only secondary specialized education.
7. Komarov, Ekonomicheskie problemy, quotes a thirteenfold increase of scientists; this does not tally with the figure given by V. M.
Buzuev in Naselenie, trudovye resursy SSSR, ed. D. I. Valentei and
I. F. Sorokina (Moscow: Mysl', 1971), p. 281. Using 1968 statistics,
and specifying which persons should be regarded as scientific workers,
Buzuev quotes an increase of 8.8 times over 1940. The official statistical yearbook, Narodnoe khoziaistvo SSSR v 1972 g. (Moscow: Statis-
tika), p. 506, gives an increase of 281 percent for the total labor
force between 1940 and 1972, and 982 percent for those engaged in
scientific work and its servicing.

8. Instruction of the Council of Ministers of the USSR, dated April 26, 1974. Several other universities were opened in 1974; see N. S. Egorov, "Reshaia zadachi, postavlennye partiei," Vestnik vysshei shkoly, no. 9 (1974): 3.

9. Komarov, Ekonomicheskie problemy, pp. 112-13, 143-44.

10. T. R. Zarikhta and I. N. Nazimov, Ratsional'noe ispol'zovanie trudovykh resursov molodezhi (Moscow: Ekonomika, 1970), pp. 154-56.

11. G. F. Panachin, "Povyshenie kvalifikatsii uchitelei—velenie vremeni," Sovetskaia pedagogika, no. 2 (1974): 16.

12. V. N. Turchenko, "Nauchno-tekhnicheskaia revolutsiia i problemy obrazovaniia," Voprosy filosofii, no. 2 (1973): 25; V. Krasil'-nikov, letter to the editor of Literaturnaia gazeta, May 15, 1974, p. 13.

13. A. A. Astakhov and V. F. Semenov, Kapital'nye vlozheniia v vysshuiu shkolu (Moscow: Vysshaia shkola, 1972), pp. 72-73.

14. E. Slastenko, "Integratsiia vuzov," Voprosy ekonomiki, no. 4 (1974): 147-48.

15. V. Kostakov, "Zaniatost' naseleniia v usloviiakh intensifikatsii proizvodstva," Voprosy ekonomiki, no. 4 (1974): 37.

16. V. I. Staroverov, Gorod ili derevnia (Moscow: Politizdat, 1972), p. 76.

17. A. Dadashev, "O povyshenii effektivnosti ispol'zovaniia trudovykh resursov," Voprosy ekonomiki, no. 4, (1974): p. 122.

18. Kostakov, "Zaniatost' naseleniia," p. 44, n. 4; the figure is calculated from the 1970 census.

19. W. R. Bohning, The Migration of Workers in the United King-dom and the European Community, (Oxford: Oxford University Press, 1972), pp. 126-27.

20. Up to 48 days in some industries, according to F. Seliukov, "Sotsial'nye problemy upravleniia," Voprosy ekonomiki, no. 2 (1974): 123.

21. T. M. Afanas'eva, Ranniaia orientatsiia ili pozdnii samo-analiz? (Moscow: Molodaia gvardiia, 1972), p. 19; L. Ananich and L. Bliakhman, Zavodskaia molodezh': professional'nye interesy (Moscow: Molodaia gvardiia, 1971), pp. 118ff.; Vasil'eva, Sotsial'no-professional'nyi uroven', pp. 72-92.

V. N. Moskovich, "Podgotovka i perepodgotovka kvalifitsirovan-nykh rabochikh," in Osnovnye problemy ratsional'nogo ispol'zovaniia trudovykh resursov SSSR, ed. E. L. Manevich (Moscow: Nauka, 1971), p. 285, adduces a table showing that the number of workers (except in agriculture) had risen by 42.7 percent between 1960 and 1969, while the number of those who had had on-the-job training had risen by 60.2 percent, so some must have undergone more than one training.

22. Ananich and Bliakhman, Zavodskaia molodezh', p. 42.

23. N. I. Bondarenko, "O sisteme podgotovki uchitelei trudovogo obucheniia," Sovetskaia pedagogika, no. 1 (1974): 77-78.

24. Panachin, "Povyshenie kvalifikatsii uchitelei," pp. 14, 17.

25. Ministry of Higher and Secondary Specialized Education, Instruktivnoe pis'mo, no. 34 (June 17, 1974).

26. E. A. Klimov, "Psikhologiia professii," Professional'no-tekhnicheskoe obrazovanie, nos. 11, 12 (1973), and no. 1 (1974).

27. N. A. Aminov, "Funktsional'nye sostoianiia pri monotonnoi rabote i balans osnovnykh nervnykh protsessov," Voprosy psikhologii, no. 2 (1974): 77-83.

28. K. M. Gurevich, Professional'naia prigodnost' i osnovnye svoistva nervnoi sistemy (Moscow: Nauka, 1970), chapters 4, 5.

29. N. P. Kuzin, "Nekotorye itogi deiatel'nosti Akademii pedagogicheskikh nauk SSSR za 1972 g.," Sovetskaia pedagogika, no. 6 (1973): 8-16.

30. A report on this conference appeared in Voprosy psikhologii, no. 3 (1973): 169-70, but I was unable to obtain the actual papers, which were published under the title Psikhofiziologicheskie osnovy professional'nogo otbora (Kiev: Naukova dumka, 1973).

31. For example, by A. Tsiko, "Ob istinnom i lozhnom samoutverzhdenii lichnosti," Literaturnaia gazeta, July 3, 1974, p. 13.

3

THE SOCIOLOGY OF
SOVIET HIGHER EDUCATION:
A REVIEW OF RECENT
EMPIRICAL RESEARCH
George Avis

The interaction between society and education has been an important avenue of Soviet sociological inquiry since the reestablishment of
sociology as an independent discipline in the USSR in the late 1950s.
Students of Soviet society in the West have been introduced via translations, commentaries, and frequent citations in sociological literature
to the results of the first major empirical investigations in this field,
particularly those examining the attitudes and aspirations of young
people of school age. Relatively less attention has been directed toward the considerable volume of Soviet empirical research into the
social aspects of higher education. Yet the development of such
research in the last eight to ten years has been remarkably rapid. [1]
Indeed, a recently published collection of research papers contained
contributions from no less than 8 research institutes, 14 universities,
and 33 higher technical and pedagogical institutes. [2]

Until the mid-1960s Soviet sociologists appear to have taken comparatively little interest in the problems of higher education as such. [3]
With a few exceptions, the empirical studies undertaken before this
were limited to isolated, often amateurish, localized surveys conducted
within individual higher education institutions (VUZy) for mainly administrative and pedagogical purposes. By 1965, research of a more professional nature and on a larger scale had commenced in several major
VUZy. A significant stimulus to this research was provided by the setting up in January 1967 of the Laboratory of Sociological Research on
Problems of Student Upbringing within Leningrad's Institute of Complex
Social Research. The functions assigned to it by the Ministry of Higher
and Secondary Specialized Education of the Russian Republic were:

1. To conduct concrete sociological research into student life, the
role of public organizations in student upbringing, and ways of establishing student self-management.
2. To coordinate similar research being conducted in other VUZy.

3. To organize the collection and dissemination of the results of research into problems of student upbringing. [4]

Major projects developed in the universities of Gorky, Rostov, Moscow, Novosibirsk, Sverdlovsk, Tartu, and Voronezh, as well as in other specialized VUZy in Moscow, Perm, Tomsk, Kaunas, and elsewhere. Particular emphasis in these projects was given to the social aspects of selection and recruitment to VUZy, the social class composition of students, the process of teaching and upbringing, academic and personal development, failure and dropout. [5]

It is the aim of this essay to examine the published results of research on some of these topics, giving special emphasis to studies relating to the impact of social class on the selection and performance of full-time VUZ students. What follows is not intended to be a thoroughgoing review of the literature but merely a preliminary exploration, so any conclusions we have drawn must be regarded as tentative.

STUDENT SELECTION AND ENROLLMENT

The transition from secondary to tertiary education in the life of young people has been the object of detailed investigation by Soviet sociologists and educationists in recent years. There may be several reasons for this. Higher education plays a crucial role in future Soviet economic, scientific, and technological development and is a key factor in social and occupational mobility. The turmoil created by the failure of the 1958 educational reforms and the demand for higher education from ever-increasing cohorts of secondary school graduates have heightened public awareness of the social problems involved in highly selective VUZ recruitment. And, generally, the attention of sociologists has been attracted more and more to the study of the attitudes, aspirations, and behavior of the younger generation, including students.

Soviet researchers have adopted the traditional modes of inquiry in this area. Sociodemographic variables (age, social class, residence, parental education) that characterize applicants and entrants to different types of VUZ and faculty have been contrasted, and these in turn compared with the distribution of the same variables in the population at large; the orientation of young people toward higher education and influences on specialty choice have been exhaustively examined; and studies have been made of the reliability and validity of procedures for selecting VUZ entrants.

The existence of systematic differences between various social groups in regard to access to higher education has been confirmed by many Soviet sociological studies. The close association between the social origins of school children and their intentions to go on to higher education appears to persist through to the stage of application to specific VUZy. Table 3.1 illustrates the considerable preponderance of

TABLE 3.1

Social Origins of VUZ Applicants, 1966-69
(percent)

Institutions	Number	Specialists	Employees	Manual Workers	Peasants	Other
Leningrad University (1967)	784	30.5	38.4[a]	25.8	2.2	4.4
Leningrad VUZy (1968-69)	6270	39.4	11.7	32.0	9.3	7.6
Rostov University (1966)	n.a.[b]	27.1	57.7		15.2	—
Rostov VUZy (1966)	2823	21.2	66.7		12.1	—
Voronezh University (1968)[c]	n.a.		52.3	39.1	8.6	—
Novosibirsk University (1968)	n.a.	51.0	12.5	26.0	2.6	7.9
USSR Population 1968		22.9		54.8	22.27	0.03

[a]Includes 13.3 percent children of military personnel.
[b]n.a.—not available.
[c]Includes applicants by social origins or own social status (social group/class affiliation).

Sources: Zhuravleva and Sikevich, "Sotsial'naia obuslovlennost'," p. 57 (Leningrad University); Zhuravleva, "Nekotorye voprosy," p. 191 (Leningrad VUZy); Rubin and Kolesnikov, Student, p. 70 (Rostov University) and pp. 65-66 (Rostov VUZy); Rakhmanin, "Sotsiologicheskie issedovaniia," p. 90 (Voronezh); Liss, "Ob ustoichivosti," p. 34 (Novosibirsk); Mervyn Matthews, Class and Society in Soviet Russia (London: Allen Lane, 1972), p. 35 (USSR population). Full citation of sources in notes at end of chapter.

children of highly qualified nonmanual workers among applicants to a
number of large universities and groups of VUZy. The proportion of applicants from manual workingclass backgrounds consistently falls well
below the proportion of manual workers in the Soviet population as a
whole, while peasant children would appear to be reluctant to apply at
all.

The differences between the various VUZy are presumably accounted
for by the demographic makeup of the populations from which they recruit, the composition of the samples, and the different degrees of
prestige of the institutions. Thus, the figures for children of specialists
are particularly high in the major scientific and industrial centers of
Leningrad and Novosibirsk, while the smaller cities of Voronezh and
Rostov clearly attract peasant applicants from a large rural catchment
area. However, census data for the social class composition of relevant oblast' populations suggest initial impressions may be too crude. [6]
Thus, the proportion of manual workers in Leningrad, Rostov, and Novosibirsk regions is well above the national average, and consequently
the representation of this class among VUZ applicants is even less favorable than the figures in Table 3.1 indicate. Moreover, the proportions of children from peasant families applying to Leningrad VUZy and
Rostov University are equal to or higher than the percentage of peasants
in the respective oblast' populations. On the other hand, peasant children are seriously underrepresented among applicants to Voronezh and
Novosibirsk universities. It is clear that these local divergences from
the general pattern call for a more subtle analysis based on further
research.

When one looks at the level of parental education for these applicants, similar disproportions are observed. In his study at Novosibirsk
University, Liss found that nearly one-third of fathers and more than
one-fifth of mothers of the applicants were themselves VUZ graduates,
and a further 34 to 37 percent and 37 to 39 percent, respectively, had
received a full secondary or post-secondary education. Comparing his
results with 1959 census statistics and with Shubkin's 1966 data on the
parents of Novosibirsk secondary school graduates, he concluded that
the proportions of parents in highly qualified occupations and with specialist education were appreciably higher among VUZ applicants than
among either of the other two populations. [7] Moreover, from 1966 to
1970 the social class composition of Novosibirsk University applicants
remained more or less stable. [8] The survey of applicants to three faculties of Leningrad University in 1967 revealed that nearly 40 percent of
their parents had received higher education, and another 21.9 percent,
secondary specialized education. [9] The representation of various social
groups among the Rostov University applicants, although obscured by
the statistical grouping together of employees and manual workers, appears to be less unbalanced, but even here some 49 percent of all
parents had full secondary or higher education qualifications. [10] Analogous results are reported in studies at other Soviet VUZy. [11]

If the children of nonmanual workers are overrepresented among those who attempt to gain admission to VUZy, the imbalance becomes even more marked among successful entrants. [12] Interpretation of much empirical research on this problem is frustrated by lack of overall relevant data for Soviet VUZy and of details of their catchment areas, as well as by the frequent use of crude occupational categories and confusion of social origins and status. Nevertheless, some of the available data from various studies have been summarized in Table 3.2 in order to give a broad illustration of the social class composition of university students in the mid-1960s. The figures highlight the existence of what Soviet sociologists acknowledge to be "factual inequality" (as distinct from legal equality) of educational opportunity at the tertiary level. Generally speaking, the proportion of students with parents employed in nonmanual occupations is two to three times greater than the proportion of this occupational category in the population at large, whereas the children of manual workers and peasants are very much underrepresented. Applicants with a specialist or employee background usually compete more efficiently in the entrance examinations than those from the other social groups and hence tend to predominate even more among successful entrants. Thus, whereas their percentage among applicants to Voronezh University in 1968 amounted to 52.3 (See Table 3.1), they comprised 58.3 percent of the eventual enrollment, while the corresponding figures for manual workingclass applicants show a decrease from 39.1 percent to 31.4 percent. More dramatically, specialists' children who applied to Rostov University in the peak year of 1966* increased their representation in this way from 27.1 percent to 50.4 percent. Unlike their workingclass peers, the children of kolkhoz peasants quite often hold their own in the entrance competition. It seems likely that, other considerations apart, rural secondary school graduates appraise their chances of VUZ admission realistically (that is, pessimistically), so that comparatively few bother to apply. Those who do so are usually above average in ability and determination.

The increased percentages of nonmanuals in 1965 and 1966 are due to the removal of the pre-VUZ work experience requirement. Before then, the bulk of students were admitted as former production workers (proizvodstvenniki) whose social class was classified by their own social status rather than by social origin. Some VUZy still take in a large number of such recruits. This, coupled with the unavailability of full admissions data for later years, makes it difficult to discern trends in student social class composition. More recent figures suggest that, for universities, the differential distribution of various social groups in the student body has not altered substantially. In 1969, for

---

*This was a peak year because in order to dismantle Khrushchev's reform the government decreed that all pupils in grades 10 and 11 should graduate from school that year.

TABLE 3.2

Social Class Composition of Students in
Selected State Universities, By Year
(percent)

Social Group (or background)	Gorky	Kharkov	Urals (Sverdlovsk)	Rostov	Voronezh	Latvian
1965						
Specialists and Employees	60.0	70.0	38.0	62.9	n.a.	60.0
Manual Workers	36.0	22.8	19.0	31.7	n.a.	32.0
Peasants	4.0	7.3	n.a.	5.4	n.a.	8.0
1966						
Specialists and Employees	65.0	68.0	66.0	74.1	67.3	n.a.
Manual Workers	30.0	25.4	28.4	22.3	27.3	n.a.
Peasants	5.0	6.6	0.7	3.2	5.4	n.a.
1967						
Specialists and Employees	65.0	55.0	n.a.	62.4	59.6	n.a.
Manual Workers	30.0	30.6	n.a.	33.6	24.7	n.a.
Peasants	5.0	15.0	n.a.	4.0	15.7	n.a.
1968						
Specialists and Employees	n.a.	n.a.	52.5	n.a.	58.3	47.7
Manual Workers	n.a.	n.a.	43.7	n.a.	31.4	40.6
Peasants	n.a.	n.a.	3.8	n.a.	10.3	11.7

Note: Data for Gorky and Latvian Universities refer to all students; the rest, to first-year students.

Sources: For Gorky, Mishin, "Problema," p. 9; for Kharkov, V. I. Astakhova, "Osnovnye tendentsii izmeneniia sotsial'noi struktury studenchestva," in Effektivnost', ed. Leonavichius, p. 10; for Urals, Rutkevich and Filippov, Sotsial'nye, pp. 135-36, and Klassy, sotsial'nye sloi i gruppy v SSSR, ed. Ts. A. Stepanian and V. S. Semenov (Moscow: Nauka, 1968), pp. 210-11; for Rostov, Rubin and Kolesnikov, Student, p. 70 and A. V. Isaiko, "Nekotorye sotsial'nye problemy vysshego i vechernego obrazovaniia," in Effektivnost', ed. Leonavichius, p. 224; for Voronezh, Rakhmanin, "Sotsiologicheskie issledovaniia," p. 87; for Latvian, M. E. Ashmane, "Izuchenie tendentsii izmeneniia sotsial'noi struktury studenchestva vysshikh uchebnykh zavedenii i uchashchikhsia srednikh spetsial'nykh uchebnykh zavedenii LSSR," in Sotsial'nye problemy truda i obrazovaniia, ed. M. E. Ashmane et al. (Riga, 1969), vyp 3, p. 18. Full citation of sources in notes at end of chapter.

example, the share of students of nonmanual background in the Perm, Belorussian, and Urals universities totaled 52, 55, and 52 percent, respectively. [13]

Universities, however, comprise only a small proportion of all Soviet VUZy. A more accurate picture of student social class composition may be obtained by looking at other types of VUZ. Table 3.3 presents available data for three large groups of VUZy, each of which contains a university and several higher technical and other specialized institutes. These figures, when compared with those in Table 3.2, suggest that the manual worker group is somewhat better represented among students of nonuniversity institutions of higher education, especially when these are situated in industrialized urban areas.

Other isolated data confirm the overall situation. In a sample of five Leningrad VUZy in 1968, the student body contained 52.7 percent of nonmanuals (including 42 percent children of specialists) and 29.8 percent of workers' children. [14] The corresponding percentages for enrollments in all Leningrad VUZy in 1969 were 52 and 44.5 percent, [15] although Latvian VUZy show an increase of workers' children among entrants from 34.3 percent in 1969 to 40.6 percent in 1970. [16]

Certainly the general trend appears to be that the representation of manual workers increased slightly in the late 1960s while that of peasants continued to decline steadily. Nevertheless, the overall share of students from worker and peasant families in Soviet VUZy remained low enough by 1969 to cause considerable official concern and to prompt such measures as the creation of preparatory departments to improve their representation.

Social class seems to be linked, too, with preference for the particular specialty taught within a VUZ. Children of workers more often choose to go to institutions offering technical or applied science specialties, and those of specialists and employees prefer the pure sciences and humanities. Thus, in Sverdlovsk, students of manual workingclass origins were found to predominate in the institutes of mining, railway engineering, and forestry; the children of nonmanual workers, on the other hand, provided the largest proportion of students in the university, the conservatoire, and in the polytechnical, pedagogical, architectural, and medical institutes. [17] A broadly similar pattern also is to be observed in the part-time divisions of these VUZy. There is evidence, moreover, that within a given VUZ, whether university or specialized institute, certain faculties tend to attract more recruits from one particular social group than from others. In Ufa Aviation Institute, students of nonmanual origins are in the overwhelming majority in the departments of industrial electronics, aviation instrumentation, and production automation and mechanization (that is, the most prestigious and interesting specialties) but appear to be much less attracted to production welding or machine-tool technology. [18] Such patterns of specialty choice may reflect both class differences in assimilation of occupational values and a process of self-screening by potential

TABLE 3.3

Social Class Composition of Full-Time Students,
By Year and Groups of VUZy
(percent)

Social Group (or background)	USSR	Latvian Republic	Sverdlovsk Region	Gorky City
1965-66				
Specialists and Employees	75.4	41.7	44.9	n.a.
Manual Workers	24.6	38.5	50.0	n.a.
Peasants		19.8	5.3	n.a.
1966-67				
Specialists and Employees	n.a.	52.6	46.1	58.0
Manual Workers	n.a.	33.4	48.6	31.0
Peasants	n.a.	14.0	5.3	11.0
1967-68				
Specialists and Employees	77.3	51.7	49.7	56.0
Manual Workers	22.6	36.6	45.3	36.0
Peasants		11.7	5.0	8.0
1968-69				
Specialists and Employees	22.9	46.8	50.5	n.a.
Manual Workers	54.8	40.3	44.6	n.a.
Peasants	22.3	12.9	4.9	n.a.
1969-70				
Specialists and Employees	23.9	52.3	50.7	n.a.
Manual Workers	54.5	34.3	45.3	n.a.
Peasants	21.6	13.4	4.0	n.a.

Note: Sverdlovsk data refer to all students, the rest to first-year students.

Sources: For Sverdlovsk region, Rutkevich and Filippov, Sotsial'nye, p. 131; for Gorky city, Mishin, "Problema," p. 10; for Latvia, Ashmane, "Sotsial'nyi sostav," p. 17; for USSR population, Zev Katz, Patterns of Social Stratification in the USSR (Cambridge, Mass.: Center for International Studies, MIT, 1973), p. 3, and Matthews, Class and Society, p. 35. Full citation of sources in notes at end of chapter.

students as they attempt to match their aspirations to their chances of acceptance. [19] Indeed, it would seem quite feasible to construct a typology of Soviet VUZy according to location, degree of selectivity, admissions standards, and specialties taught, and to examine the distribution of social groups among the students and their access to staff and material resources.

The parents of Soviet students have significantly better educational qualifications than parents in general. This fact lends support to the claim of some Soviet sociologists that educational level provides as reliable an indicator of social group membership as occupation. As Liss observes: "A family's education contains within itself the essence of the specific social circumstances of the individual's development, and this strengthens its differentiating function."[20] Others, however, are at pains to point out that, although a sizeable proportion of Soviet students may not be experiencing intergenerational mobility, the majority are in fact climbing higher up the educational and occupational ladder than their parents. [21] The evidence is that the overall proportion of second-generation VUZ students probably varies between one-fifth and one-third. But it can rise to as high as 40 to 50 percent or more in certain institutes and faculties, thus creating an embarrassing degree of intelligentsia self-recruitment. [22]

The argument that inadequacies in the cultural background of the home largely account for educational inequality is a familiar one. Of course, it may be used to divert attention from more fundamental inequalities of income and power. To what extent do the economic circumstances of a Soviet child's family affect his chances of obtaining higher education? Researchers frequently refer in vague terms to the disincentive of temporary economic inequalities during the present stage of the building of communism, but dismiss the idea that income differential is one of them since higher education in the Soviet Union is free. Detailed empirical investigation in this area, however, is uncommon. In her impressive longitudinal study of Leningrad secondary school graduates, Vasil'eva found that only 12 percent of her sample cited financial circumstances for not entering full-time higher education and, more significant, that 72 percent of pupils in this group were fatherless. Significantly fewer children from single-parent homes went on to full-time higher education after graduating from school, and they were also less likely to enroll in part-time courses. A similar finding was made in respect to pupils from families with three or more children, irrespective of social class. [23] Minkina and her associates at Gorky University provide some revealing evidence on the practice of hiring private tutors to prepare for entrance examinations. About 20 percent of the 1967 intake had received private coaching. Not unexpectedly, nearly a quarter of those admitted with employee and specialist parents had employed a coach, compared with only 5 percent of workers' children. The problem is seen not merely as cultural but as moral, too, since specialists are better able to afford tutoring fees. [24] On the other hand, Zhuravleva could find no strong link between an applicant's material circumstances and his chances of gaining admission.[25] It would be reasonable to assume that rural school graduates are more often called upon to sacrifice further study in order to contribute family income. This would partly explain their poor application record. Other research relating to income and student performance at VUZ will be treated below.

There is now extensive documentation demonstrating that the economic, social, and cultural disparities between urban and rural areas in the Soviet Union have a strong impact on the higher education opportunities of young people. What remains to be established by empirical research is whether place of residence is more significant here than social class membership. By definition, of course, kolkhoz peasants are rural dwellers, but so too are members of other social groups such as sovkhoz (state farm) workers. What, for example, are the latter's chances of acquiring higher education compared to those of peasants? Are the chances of country children improved if they live near an urban center? What educational disadvantages are suffered by industrial workers who live in semirural settlements? There is a lack of detailed studies on the association between higher education and place of residence that discriminate clearly between such groups.[26] Certainly Soviet peasants generally lag far behind the rest of the population in the sphere of higher education—a phenomenon causing much current concern. But disparities also exist between urban dwellers. Researchers have yet to examine whether the features of poor schooling and restricted cultural amenities accounting for rural dwellers' inadequate record may not apply as well to, say, workingclass areas in big cities.[27]

Numerous investigations have been made by sociologists into social differences in occupational values among school children, most of them demonstrating a strong statistical relationship between aspirations for higher education and social class origins. More recently, interesting work has been done by Titma on the transmission of such values within socially homogeneous and heterogeneous families.[28] The way in which VUZ applicants and students themselves evaluate the influences on their choice of course has been the subject of several studies. In surveys of applicants to Rostov and Leningrad universities in 1966 and 1967, respondents most often cited the mass media as an important influence (45 percent and 53 percent, respectively), then school or teacher (33 percent and 36 percent); family influence was mentioned by only one-fifth of Rostov applicants, and in Leningrad it appears to be replaced more often by advice from "specialists in the chosen field" (16.9 percent).[29] Similarly, only 20 percent of a huge sample of students in Sverdlovsk (N=7, 931) considered their family to be a factor in their decision to study at VUZ.[30]

It would appear that Soviet students generally are motivated more by school, television, radio, and literature than by their parents. We have a little evidence on the way social class differences affect the strength of parental influence. In their study of student attitudes in various pedagogical institutes and universities in Moscow, Minsk,

Novosibirsk, and Odessa, Gurova and Rychkova show that family influence on course choice was placed higher than that of either teachers or mass media (38, 33, and 31 percent, respectively)—a reflection perhaps of the home backgrounds from which these humanities VUZy tend to attract their recruits. [31] Interestingly, peer influence is markedly weak in all these studies. Finally, in a piece of research at Gorky University, student response on this question was directly compared to social class origins (see Table 3. 4). It is evident that the influence of parents here is strongest in the group of nonmanual origins. Peasants' and workers' children, however, received advice about their careers in higher education mainly at school. These findings tend to confirm claims that social class differences in student enrollment may be attributed to differences in the cultural climate and traditions of applicants' home backgrounds.

During the early Soviet period, VUZ admissions policy was deliberately regulated to ensure that the less-privileged were fairly represented. Nowadays, cultural inequalities restricting educational opportunity are regarded by Soviet sociologists as a consequence of economic inequalities that are an inevitable feature of the socialist stage of development. If the latter are to be eradicated, the priorities of national economic and scientific progress must govern recruitment and training in Soviet higher education. Admissions therefore are strictly controlled by a system of competitive examinations designed to produce the best recruits in the right numbers for each specialty. As an increasing proportion of young people from culturally "disadvantaged" homes receives sufficient secondary education to undertake further studies, more attention is being paid to the operation of selection procedures and their impact on the social composition of enrollments. Available research has called into question the validity and reliability of VUZ entrance examinations both as indicators of past school performance and as predictors of future academic success. [32] They have been criticized particularly for their rigidity and overemphasis on academic knowledge—a feature likely to favor candidates from cultured homes and good schools. Nor do existing selection methods elucidate nonintellectual qualities that might be just as important for the successful completion of the predominantly vocational and sociopolitical training offered by Soviet VUZy, and that may be more strongly developed in children of workers and peasants. [33] Considerable concern has been voiced at the evidence showing frequent rejection of talented applicants, subsequent dropout of entrants, and the relative lack of firm vocational orientation among even final-year students in VUZy. Such criticisms seem to echo, if faintly, the charges of cultural bias and irrelevance made against the use of intelligence and attainment tests in the West.

An interesting thesis on this topic is propounded by the economist I. N. Kozyrev, who claims that the social structure of student intakes is directly determined by the ratio of applicants to vacant places, that is, by the intensity of the entrance competition—the more severe the

TABLE 3.4

Influence on Course Choice of Students, By Social Origin
(percent)

| | Most Important Influence (percent of students) | | | |
Social Origin	Parents	School	Friends	Own Choice
Children of manual workers	9.6	52.4	9.5	28.5
Children of peasants	—	66.7	—	33.3
Children of employees and Intelligentsia	27.8	33.3	5.6	33.3

Note: Details of sample not available. Columns add horizontally to 100 percent.

Source: T. A. Lependina et al., "Zavisimost' uspevaemosti ot sostava studentov," in Sotsiologicheskie issledovaniia, ed. Levin, p. 44. Full citation of source in notes at end of chapter.

competition is, the greater will be the proportion of specialists and
employees (and their children) in the eventual enrollment, as was the
case in 1966, the peak year for the number of applicants to VUZy.
Although his data are not entirely convincing, he does throw light on
how an uncontrolled and outdated pattern of public demand for higher
education runs counter to national economic requirements. The official
policy of increasing places in industrial VUZy failed to alter the traditional preferences of applicants for popular specialties and "prestigious"
institutions. Competition to enroll in the latter remains severe, but
the relative proportion of applicants to industrial VUZy has dropped.
And since employee and specialist candidates perform better in intense
competition, they are more strongly represented in the student bodies
of popular VUZy. [34]

ACADEMIC PERFORMANCE AND FAILURE

Although the familiar indexes of social class—parental education,
father's occupation and income, material circumstances, size of family,
and so on—have been shown by Soviet researchers to be strongly linked
to school achievement, occupational values, and chances of VUZ entrance, their influence on student academic performance is less clear.
It must be borne in mind that student status is normally characterized
by a certain degree of independence from family. Moreover, since
students are generally of proven superior ability, they constitute a
select group in which the influence of social class should be considerably reduced. This is certainly the conclusion of much British
research. [35]

The Soviet literature on performance in higher education has been
more concerned with low achievers than high achievers. Much of the
research on low performance and wastage among students, however,
fails to explore in depth factors underlying academic failure. Unlike
their Western colleagues, for instance, Soviet sociologists rarely attempt to investigate the effect of psychological and social-psychological
variables in this area. Student failure is attributed primarily to inadequate schooling, faulty selection, or poor motivation. At the same time,
much data have been collected on the association between performance
and such factors as urban/rural background, type of schooling, accommodation, material circumstances, and social class.

Students from rural areas, although disadvantaged by previous
mediocre schooling, appear to be more assiduous and eventually to
achieve better results than their urban peers. Surveys in Kaunas polytechnical and medical institutes revealed that rates of unsatisfactory
academic progress and failure were highest among students from large
towns and lowest among ex-rural dwellers. [36] Iatsechko found that
twice as many rural as urban students in Gorky University dropped out

in their first year, but by the third and fourth years they were achieving higher average marks. Interestingly, he is more inclined to blame short-comings in the university's teaching and counseling methods than external factors.[37] By contrast, one of the few correlational studies we have examined could find no statistically significant relationship between performance and urban or rural schooling in a small sample of teacher trainees.[38]

The necessity of undertaking casual employment to supplement their stipends is not uncommon for Soviet students from less well-off families. Evidence of social class differences in the degree of material support from parents is cited by Aitov. Among students in Ufa, such support was received by 83 percent of those with parents in nonmanual occupations, by 70 percent of manual workers' children, and by only 31 percent of peasant students. It is true that a higher percentage of the latter social groups enjoy stipends; nevertheless, more of them are compelled to get extra money by working part time: peasants—47 percent, workers—37.9 percent, and employees—22.2 percent.[39] Conflicting findings are reported by other researchers. On the one hand, we learn that the impact of part-time work on academic progress of Rostov medical students is statistically significant,[40] and that Moscow students from families with both the lowest and highest income per head performed worst of all;[41] on the other hand, course marks obtained by Sverdlovsk students from families in the very same income categories were higher on average.[42]

A greater degree of consistency occurs in Soviet findings on the connection between place of residence and academic success. About one in eight dropouts blames failure specifically on inadequate accommodation.[43] Most studies suggest that performance, in terms of drop-out rates and course marks, is harmed by residence in privately rented rooms and flats. Students living in hostels or at home are obviously less encumbered by domestic chores and generally enjoy more comfortable living conditions and better study facilities. Gromov and his associates in Rostov, for instance, found a positive correlation between course marks and residence at home—and this held true even for married students living with their parents.[44] Other findings give the edge to residence in student hostels, with their supportive collective spirit as the factor most closely associated with academic success.[45] Typically, the statistical data examined here do not deal with the considerable number of students whose individual fates belie the above trends. Unfortunately, the simple descriptive statistics employed at present in much Soviet sociological research are inadequate tools for investigating complex social phenomena.

The variable of social class per se appears to have an indirect effect of limited duration on performance in higher education. Differences in rates of dropping out among students of different social origins are certainly to be observed. Liss reports that one-third of the students of Novosibirsk University whose parents were manual workers dropped out during the years 1966-68, compared with a quarter of those from non-manual backgrounds. He maintains that "this testifies to the fact that the social circumstances of the individual's earlier development leave their mark on his success at the higher school to the degree that they are reflected in the extent of his preparation for higher education."[46] But these overall figures mask the chronology of wastage. It is generally accepted that dropping out occurs mainly during the first and second years of the normal five-year course. Since the children of workers are less well equipped both academically and culturally on entry, they are in greatest danger of failing during the period of adaptation to VUZ life. Consequently, the evidence shows that they are substantially overrepresented among first-year dropouts compared to their fellow students from nonmanual and peasant backgrounds. However, other data on both low and high achievement suggest that the initial association between social class and performance operates in favor of the worker and peasant groups in the later stages of a course.[47] It might reasonably be inferred that students of nonmanual origins enjoy certain academic and cultural advantages initially but fail to exploit them, and that nonintellectual qualities of persistence, application, and strong vocational orientation probably account for the relatively better subsequent performance of the other groups. In this connection, it may be indicative that, in two correlational studies using samples of senior students, no significant relationship between social class and course performance was established.[48]

VOCATIONAL ORIENTATION AND SOCIOPOLITICAL TRAINING

The approach of Soviet educationists to the social, moral, and personal development of students differs fundamentally from that typically found in Western universities and colleges. The product of a Soviet VUZ is intended to be both a dedicated, innovative specialist in a particular branch of production and a socially mature and ideologically aware leader of men—a true model of the "new communist man." Specific programs of sociopolitical training are laid down to ensure that he assimilates the necessary skills, attitudes, and values to fulfill these roles on graduation. (Such training includes participation in political education and propaganda work, voluntary labor, and other social tasks both within VUZy and at enterprises and collective farms.) In particular, he is expected to develop a strong orientation toward his future profession and to participate in student political, cultural, and social activities.

This official notion of upbringing (vospitanie) in Soviet higher education reflects a narrow vocationalism; the student role is part and parcel of the occupational role. Whether, in fact, there exists a real correspondence between the content of VUZ curriculums and the content of work actually performed by specialists is debatable. It certainly cannot be assumed that young people themselves see these roles in the same light. Indeed, there is convincing evidence that their expectations, attitudes, and values may diverge considerably from officially approved ones. We have already seen that the nature of popular demand for higher education may conflict with national economic needs; the same may be said of students' attitudes to their chosen specialties and to sociopolitical training.

Soviet educationists have expressed great concern in recent times at the inadequate vocational orientation of VUZ students. Many secondary school graduates regard higher education and student status as an end in itself, a social value to be consumed, rather than as a preparation for a specific occupation. But the strength of vocational orientation has not been a major criterion for student selection. In their Leningrad University study, therefore, Zhuravleva and Sikevich employed a standardized interview schedule to assess the applicants' knowledge of and interest in their preferred course of study. Overall, these proved to be less than satisfactory. More disturbingly, of applicants who were eventually admitted into the university, nearly half were inadequately acquainted with the occupation they were to train for, and about one in five had obviously chosen a course quite at random. [49] Similarly, in Ufa, Khairullin found among a sample of 4, 957 applicants to VUZy that only 23. 6 percent had any sense of vocation for their chosen specialty, and two-fifths simply wanted to be students. [50]

The absence of genuine vocational orientation at the selection stage means, in effect, that VUZy are faced with the unfamiliar and ambiguous task of providing vocational guidance to students who have already formally committed themselves to specific careers. Many studies of student attitudes testify to the academic difficulties, personal disillusionment, and dropout of such students when they encounter the realities of specialized studies and industrial practice on course. Oparev, for instance, questioned some 1, 660 final-year students in 13 VUZy, including two universities and six pedagogical institutes, on their reasons for choosing their specialties and on their job intentions. Table 3. 5 summarizes his data for selected institutions. Clearly, the choice of course for large numbers of students in universities, pedagogical institutes, and agricultural academies had been "forced. " It is hardly surprising, therefore, that nearly a third of the total sample (including nearly 40 percent of the teacher trainees and 27 percent of the university students) had decided to reject their specialty as a career. [51]

Similar results were obtained in a 1969 survey in Leningrad University and three other VUZy in the city. Approximately one-third of the 3, 000 students in the sample, and over 40 percent of those in higher technical institutes, felt unsure of or had mistaken their vocations. Within the university, students of mathematics, physics, geology, and philosophy had the most positive attitudes toward their specialties,

TABLE 3.5

Motives for Course Choice and Job Intentions of
Final-Year Students, by Type of VUZ
(percent)

Reasons for Course Choice	Institution			
	Medical Institute	University	Pedagogical Institute	Agricultural Academy
Vocation	72.0	40.5	37.5	30.0
Simple desire to study; rejected elsewhere; sure of getting in	7.5	37.4	38.3	52.8
Near home	1.3	2.1	4.4	6.7
Example of friends	2.1	3.7	2.4	1.6
Parents' insistence	n.a.	3.5	2.2	2.6
Desire to obtain diploma or high official position; unwilling to start work	n.a.	3.4*	4.3	2.5
Other	17.1	9.4	10.9	3.8
Intend to work in specialty after graduation	86.5	73.0	61.8	83.5

*Corrected from clearly mistaken "34" in the original.

Source: Oparev, "Mnenie," pp. 24-27. Full citation of source in notes at end of chapter.

while historians, philologists, and journalists were weakest in their
vocational orientation. When these responses were analyzed by year
of course, it was found that the percentage of negative attitudes toward
the chosen specialty increased progressively from 28.6 percent among
first-year students to 43.6 percent in the final year—a deterioration the
author attributes to uninformed or overoptimistic expectations before
entry to the various courses. [52] Numerous other studies confirm these
trends, which are particularly worrying to Soviet higher education authorities. [53]

The economic and human problems whose existence is implicit in
the above findings illustrate one aspect of the dilemma that, according
to Hopper, faces the educational systems of modern industrialized
nations. Public demand for higher education must be stimulated
("warmed up") to ensure a steady supply of talented manpower to service the economy. At the same time, the ambitions and aspirations of
the less talented must be dampened down ("cooled out") to prevent
personal discontent and social conflict. Furthermore, he claims:

> the more successful an educational system is in its warming-
> up processes at a given phase in the selection process, the
> more difficult it will be to manage and conduct its cooling-
> out processes at a subsequent phase . . . . Continual tension
> and conflict are likely to surround any system's attempts to
> resolve this structural dilemma. It is a contradiction which
> is likely to generate pressures for structural change, both
> within the educational system and in the relationships of the
> system to other institutions. [54]

It may be argued that assiduous but indiscriminate official propagan-
dizing of the merits of higher education in the past has so warmed up
Soviet young people that their desire to enter a VUZ of any sort overrides
the need for careful deliberation about their future working career.
Recently introduced measures—early and more intense vocational guidance, the upgrading of technical trade schools, emphasis on the early
identification and nurturing of intellectually talented school pupils,
and the inclusion of school performance as a criterion in VUZ selection—
all these might be regarded as forms of cooling-out mechanism to
counteract the pressures of universal full secondary education on the
higher education system.

From a different point of view, it may be claimed that young adults
should be allowed more time before finally deciding on their chosen
specialty. The rapid transition of school graduates to the specialized
vocational courses in VUZy following ten or more years of general education inevitably encourages lukewarm orientation, wrong choices, and
poor performance. What may be required is greater flexibility in the
structure and functions of VUZy, and in the planning and coordination
of academic courses to facilitate interfaculty and inter-VUZ transfer.

More general programs of instruction and postponement of specialization are indeed now becoming features of Soviet higher education. [55]

The aspirations of Soviet youth for higher education are based on motives of self-fulfillment rather than on utilitarian or patriotic considerations. In general, this applies also to student attitudes to the requirements of sociopolitical training. The Rostov sociologists Rubin and Kolesnikov found that, of 600 university students who participated in sociopolitical activities, most did so to gain peer acceptance (30 percent); others to improve their cultural level (11 percent), or out of a sense of duty (23 percent), or through ideological conviction (15.4 percent), while 8 percent said "from habit." From their participation they felt they had gained: organizing skills—46.3 percent; knowledge of life—24.2 percent; moral satisfaction—17.4 percent. [56] Nonetheless, many Soviet students appear to resent, or doubt the necessity for, sociopolitical work, and up to 40 to 50 percent opt out of it. Kalits found that only about half of a large sample of Tartu University students considered that everyone should be expected to carry out such work; senior students were more negative in their attitudes than first-year respondents, and so were students of history, philology, and law, as compared with economists and physical culture students. Questioned about the usefulness of sociopolitical work, up to one-third doubted whether it broadened political outlook or provided good experience for work after graduation, and only 10 percent felt it afforded satisfaction. Again, such opinions become more negative in senior years of the course. [57] The resistance of students to sociopolitical training arises because it is too formalized, because it can conflict with the demands of academic work, and probably because it is divorced from their personal interests and aspirations. A clear indication of this is provided by the evaluation, of various desired qualities in a graduate specialist, as given by 2,300 students from nine Russian VUZy. The three most important qualities by far are seen to be a profound knowledge of the specialty, high morality, and general culture. But skills and attitudes that sociopolitical training is supposed to impart—political maturity and organizing ability—come at nearly the bottom of the poll. [58]

Finally, there is a small amount of suggestive evidence that level of participation is linked to social class. From her Sverdlovsk materials, Kniga concludes that students from families of workers and peasants were more active in sociopolitical work than children of nonmanual parents. [59] Rural students at Tartu were better disposed toward participation than their urban counterparts. [60] Among Gorky University students, parental education and the variety of sociopolitical activities undertaken at school were shown to be inversely related. [61] Conversely, a direct comparison of participation with social origins among Perm University students suggested there was little connection. [62]

CONCLUSION

The materials reviewed above have dealt primarily with educational inputs and the selective function of higher education. They attempt to answer the question: Who gets in? Such inquiries reflect a traditional concern of the sociology of education, namely, the articulation of the education system with stratification and occupational structures. Much Western research in this field rests upon tacit egalitarian assumptions—for example, that talents and abilities are randomly distributed throughout all strata of society, and that inequality of educational opportunity is socially structured. Soviet sociologists share the environmentalist viewpoint but maintain that existing inequalities in education are economically determined and will inevitably wither away.

Yet the preoccupation with social class differences in higher education characteristic of much empirical research of the late 1960s—a preoccupation that has prompted the emphasis of the present essay—and the dismay shown at the evidence of de facto inequality are difficult to explain. After all, from the point of view of Soviet class theory, the educationally privileged groups, specialists and employees, are members of the working class. Differential distribution of a value such as higher education cannot be the source of friction since social classes and groups in socialist society, unlike those of capitalist society, are equal in social relationships and nonantagonistic. This latter consideration, Soviet sociologists maintain, is crucial for a correct interpretation of superficially similar stratifying phenomena in socialist and capitalist higher education, and one that bourgeois sociologists conveniently ignore. [63] Moreover, socioeconomic differences between social classes and groups are being eliminated as Soviet society becomes increasingly more homogeneous. Why then, despite regular reference to these theoretical justifications in the literature, do Soviet researchers seem so disturbed by their own findings on social class differences? One might speculate that it is because these appear to violate basic principles of social justice or to demonstrate that the abilities and talents of workers and peasants are being left unutilized. But if so, these fears are not often stated explicitly. More fundamentally, of course, the accumulated evidence raises questions about the assumptions referred to above and reveals sociopsychological phenomena unamenable to scientific social control. Consequently, the standard formulations employed by Soviet researchers in their commentaries are sometimes embarrassingly at variance with their data.

Two conflicting approaches to the problem of class bias in higher education may be discerned in Soviet sociological studies. The first, associated with M. N. Rutkevich, stresses that the root cause of the problem is economic inequality, which can only be eradicated in the long term by economic advance; the chief priority of VUZy is to supply highly qualified personnel to do this. In the meantime, direct regulation

of the social class composition of VUZy by quotas, as in the 1920s, is
not permissible since it would contradict the legal equality of all Soviet
citizens and lower standards, just as existing admission privileges tend
to do. Intellectually bright children should receive advanced instruction
to prepare them for higher education. Rutkevich acknowledges that a
highly selective system encourages social inequalities but dismisses
them as an example of dialectical developments inevitable in the construction of communism. [64]

The contrary view is contained in the charge of elitism brought
against Rutkevich by the Gorky sociologist V. I. Mishin and his associates. He argues that the tendency of the intelligentsia to become self-
recruiting by its domination in VUZ admissions is socially divisive,
prevents the emergence of talent from other groups, and represents an
obvious injustice to young workers and peasants who might begin to
doubt the principles of equality and justice of Soviet society. The introduction of full secondary education, far from equalizing the chances of
VUZ entrance, will exacerbate the existing situation. As for the theoretical basis for the existence of inequalities, Mishin declares:

> Yes, inequality connected with payment according to labor and
> with the existence of classes is inevitable under socialism.
> But in the transitional stage from socialism to communism what
> becomes of foremost importance is the degree of inequality.
> The construction of a society with full social equality is impos-
> sible while inequality persists in important spheres of social
> life, one of which undoubtedly is the sphere of education and
> culture.

Social equality should broaden, not narrow, on the path to communism,
and this could be effected by deliberate measures to regulate the class
composition of VUZ recruits. [65]

These two viewpoints exemplify the functional contradictions of
Soviet higher education highlighted by recent anxieties about its social
composition. For decades it has served as a vehicle for the economic
and social aspirations of the Soviet people. It may not remain unchanged
if it is to reconcile these two roles in the future.

NOTES

1. For general surveys of this field see, for example: T. A. Lependina et al., "Sotsiologicheskie issledovaniia vysshei shkoly," in
Uchenye zapiski Gorkovskogo gosudarstvennogo universiteta, vyp. 100
(1970): 177-94; K. I. Mamaeva, "Nekotorye sotsiologicheskie aspekty
vysshego obrazovaniia," in Uchenye zapiski Latviiskogo gosudarstvennogo universiteta, T. 158 (1972): 3-10; V. T. Lisovskii, "Sotsiologi-

sheskie issledovaniia problem studenchestva," in Effektivnost' podgotovki spetsialistov, ed. Iu. Leonavichius et al. (Kaunas, 1969), pp.
91-94.
    2. Leonavichius et al., eds., Student v uchebnom protsesse,
(Kaunas, 1972).
    3. F. Klement, "Predmet issledovaniia—vuz," Komsomol'skaia
pravda, December 14, 1965.
    4. Lisovskii, "Sotsiologicheskie issledovaniia," p. 92. For a
detailed review of the laboratory's work see: A. V. Dmitriev, "Konkret-
nye issledovaniia problem vysshei shkoly v LGU," Vestnik Leningradskogo Universiteta: Ekonomika, Filosofiia, Pravo, no. 11, vyp. 1
(1972): 101-12.
    5. The results of much of this research are contained in the follow-
ing collections and monographs: Leonavichius, ed., Effektivnost';
Leonavichius et al., eds., Motivatsiia zhiznedeiatel'nosti studenta
(Kaunas, 1971); Molodezh' i sotsializm: Tezisy dokladov nauchno-
teoreticheskoi konferentsii (Moscow, 1967); A. Ia. Levin et al., eds.,
Sotsiologicheskie issledovaniia uchebno-vospitatel'noi raboty v vysshei
shkole (Gorky, 1969); B. I. Zelenkov et al., eds., Sotsiologicheskie
issledovaniia uchebno-vospitatel'noi raboty v vysshei shkole (Gorky,
1970); O. M. Sichivitsa, Sotsiologiia i vysshaia shkola, vol. 3 (Gorky,
1971); B. G. Anan'ev and D. A. Kerimov, eds., Chelovek i obshchestvo:
Sotsial'nye problemy molodezhi (Leningrad: Izdatel'stvo Leningradskogo
universiteta, 1969); B. G. Anan'ev, ed., Chelovek i obshchestvo:
Problemy intellektual'nogo i kul'turnogo razvitiia studenchestva (Leningrad: Izdatel'stvo Leningradskogo universiteta, 1973); S. A. Kugel' and
O. M. Nikandrov, Molodye inzhenery (Moscow: Mysl', 1971); Sotsial'-
noe prognozirovanie v oblasti obrazovaniia (Novosibirsk, 1969); M. N.
Rutkevich and F. R. Filippov, Sotsial'nye peremeshcheniia (Moscow:
Mysl', 1970); I. F. Livshits, ed., Sotsial'nye voprosy razvitiia nauki
i vysshego obrazovaniia (Tomsk: Izd. Tomskogo universiteta, 1970); B.
Rubin and Iu. Kolesnikov, Student glazami sotsiologa (Rostov: Izd.
Rostovskogo universiteta, 1968); V. T. Lisovskii, comp., Molodezh' i
obrazovanie (Moscow: Molodaia gvardiia, 1972); Leonavichius et al.,
eds., Lichnost' studenta, (Kaunas, 1970); G. M. Andreeva, ed.,
Materialy konferentsii "Kommunisticheskoe vospitanie studenchestva,"
Tartu-Kiaeriku, mai 1971g., parts I, II (Tartu: Tartuskii Gosuderstven-
nye Universitet, 1971).
    6. Itogi vsesoiuznoi perepisi naseleniia 1970 goda (Moscow: Sta-
tistika, 1973), vol. 5.
    7. L. F. Liss, "Ob ustoichivosti kharakteristik i spetsifike sotsial'-
nogo proiskhozhdeniia abiturientov universiteta," in Sotsial'noe prognozirovanie, pp. 33-43.
    8. L. F. Liss, "The Social Conditioning of Occupational Choice,"
in Social Stratification and Mobility in the USSR, ed. Murray Yanowitch
and Wesley A. Fisher (White Plains, N.Y.: International Arts and
Sciences Press, 1973), p. 279.

9. G. A. Zhuravleva and Z. V. Sikevich, "Sotsial'naia obuslovlennost' podgotovlennosti abiturienta v vuz, " in Sotsial'nye problemy, ed. Anan'ev and Kerimov, p. 57.

10. Rubin and Kolesnikov, Student, p. 64.

11. See, for example, Rutkevich and Filippov, Sotsial'nye, p. 138; V. S. Rakhmanin, "Sotsiologicheskie issledovaniia i vuzovskii uchebnyi protsess, " in Pedagogika vysshei shkoly, ed. P. M. Gaponov (Voronezh: Izd. Voronezhskogo universiteta, 1969), p. 89.

12. In her Leningrad study of secondary school graduates, Vasil'eva found that success in obtaining higher education was greater among the higher socioeconomic groups, even when school performance was held constant: E. K. Vasil'eva, Sotsial'no-professional'nyi uroven' gorodskoi molodezhi (Leningrad: Izdatel'stvo Leningradskogo universiteta, 1973), p. 42.

13. Figures for the Belorussian University are taken from S. D. Laptenok et al. , "Kontingent studentov i ikh obshchestvennaia aktivnost', " in Student, ed. Leonavichius, p. 337; for the Urals University from M. N. Rutkevich and L. I. Sennikova, "Sotsial'naia obuslovlennost' motivov postupleniia v vuz i vybora budushchei professii, " in Motivatsiia, ed. Leonavichius, p. 119; and for Perm University from V. S. Ruseikina, "Sotsial'nyi status i aktivnost' studenta, " in Uchenye zapiski Permskogo gosudarstvennogo universiteta, no. 279 (1972): 39.

14. G. A. Zhuravleva, "Nekotorye voprosy vuzovskoi orientatsii molodezhi, " in Molodezh', ed. Lisovskii, p. 191.

15. Zhuravleva, "Nekotorye voprosy, " p. 193.

16. M. E. Ashmane, "Sotsial'nyi sostav studenchestva Latviiskoi SSR, " Uchenye zapiski Latviiskogo gosudarstvennogo universiteta, T. 158 (1972): 13.

17. Rutkevich and Filippov, Sotsial'nye, p. 135. The social class composition of pedagogical institutes in several European republics of the USSR shows an overall majority of students from nonmanual backgrounds (44. 4 percent) and quite a high proportion of peasants (17. 9 percent). See S. G. Visharenko, "Ob izmeneniiakh sostava i uspevaemosti studentov pedagogicheskikh vuzov za 1958-1967 gody, " in Effektivnost', ed. Leonavichius, p. 215.

18. F. G. Khairullin, "Nekotorye problemy professional'nykh interesov molodezhi, " in Motivatsiia, ed. Leonavichius, p. 127.

19. For an interesting discussion of the implications of such a process, see Iu. N. Kozyrev, "Potrebnost' naseleniia v vysshem obrazovanii i otbor molodezhi v vuzy, " in Molodezh', ed. Lisovskii, pp. 172-82.

20. Liss, "The Social Conditioning, " pp. 285-86.

21. See, for example, M. N. Rutkevich and F. R. Filippov, "Komplektovanie studenchestva: sotsial'nye aspekty, " in Materialy, ed. Andreeva, pp. 117-18.

22. K. N. Minkina et al. , "Sotsial'naia kharakteristika studentov-pervokursnikov universiteta, " in Sotsiologicheskie issledovaniia, ed. Zelenkov, p. 23.

23. Vasil'eva, Sotsial'no-professional'nyi uroven', pp. 44-48,
67-68.

24. Minkina, "Sotsial'naia kharakteristika," pp. 23-24.

25. Zhuravleva, "Nekotorye voprosy," p. 190.

26. Zhuravleva points out that, in her sample, applicants who
lived in workers' settlements received a much higher proportion of poor
results in the entrance examination, and she calls for a special study
of this feature. Zhuravleva, "Nekotorye voprosy," p. 189.

27. Some data suggesting this might be the case were reported in
the famous Sverdlovsk study: see M. N. Rutkevich, ed., Zhiznennye
plany molodezhi (Ural'skii gos. universitet im. Gor'kogo, Sotsiologicheskie issledovaniia, Vyp. 1, Sverdlovsk, 1966).

28. M. Kh. Titma, "The Influence of Social Origins on the Occupational Values of Graduating Secondary-School Students," in Social
Stratification, ed. Yanowitch and Fisher, pp. 187-226.

29. Rubin and Kolesnikov, Student, p. 83; Zhuravleva and Sikevich,
"Sotsial'naia obuslovlennost'," p. 57.

30. Rutkevich and Sennikova, "Sotsial'naia obuslovlennost'," p.
115.

31. R. G. Gurova and G. B. Rychkova, "Orientatsiia starsheklas-
snikov na prodolzhenie obrazovaniia," in Sotsiologicheskie problemy
obrazovaniia i vospitaniia, ed. R. G. Gurova (Moscow: Pedagogika,
1973), p. 151.

32. See V. M. Iatsechko, "Uroven' znanii i uspevaemost' studentov," in Sotsiologicheskie issledovaniia, ed. Zelenkov, pp. 87-88;
A. Ia. Levin, "Nekotorye itogi izucheniia prichin neuspevaemosti studentov," in ibid., pp. 91-102; A. M. Sokhor, "Korreliatsionnyi analiz
uspevaemosti," Vestnik vysshei shkoly, no. 7 (1972): 26-30; V. G.
Zhitomirskii, "Faktory, vliiaiushchie na uspevaemost'," ibid., no. 9,
pp. 22-28.

33. Visharenko, "Ob izmeneniiakh," p. 216; Rubin and Kolesnikov,
Student, p. 220.

34. Kozyrev, "Potrebnost' naseleniia," pp. 173-82. See also
Khairullin, "Nekotorye problemy," p. 128

35. Gordon W. Miller, Success, Failure and Wastage in Higher
Education (London: University of London Institute of Education, 1970),
pp. 37-43.

36. Ch. S. Iakimavichius, "O prichinakh otseva studentov I kursa,"
in Effektivnost', ed. Leonavichius, pp. 181-84; V. M. Kuzminskis,
"O nekotorykh prichinakh neuspevaemosti studentov v Kaunasskom
Meditsinskom Institute," in Effektivnost', ed. Leonavichius, pp. 192-
95.

37. Iatsechko, "Uroven' znanii," p. 89.

38. Sokhor, "Korreliatsionnyi analiz," p. 27.

39. N. Aitov, "Sotsial'nye aspekty polucheniia obrazovaniia v
SSSR," Sotsial'nye issledovaniia, Vyp. 2, ed. N. V. Novikov et al.
(Moscow: Nauka, 1968), pp. 191, 196.

40. A. S. Gromov et al., "Vliianie sotsial'no-bytovykh faktorov na uspevaemost' studentov Rostovskogo-na-Donu meditsinskogo instituta," Sovetskoe zdravookhranenie, no. 8 (1967): 48.

41. N. M. Morozov, "Svobodnoe vremia i vsestoronnee razvitie lichnosti budushchego inzhenera," Uchenye zapiski Moskovskogo oblastnogo pedagodicheskogo instituta, T. 210, vyp. 1 (1968): 118.

42. E. M. Nezhikhovskaia, "O material'nom stimulirovanii povysheniia uspevaemosti studentov," in Student, ed. Leonavichius, pp. 289-90.

43. M. N. Rutkevich, "Why a Student Does Not Arrive at the 'Finish,'" in Contemporary Soviet Education, ed. Fred Ablin (White Plains, N.Y.: International Arts and Sciences Press, 1969), pp. 154-55.

44. Gromov, "Vliianie," p. 48.

45. T. D. Mangushev et al., "Organizatsiia uchebnogo protsessa i uspevaemost' studentov," in Sotsiologicheskie issledovaniia, ed. Levin, p. 25; Kuzminskis, "O nedotorykh," pp. 193-94.

46. Liss, "The Social Conditioning," p. 287.

47. See notes 36 and 37.

48. Sokhor, "Korreliatsionnyi," p. 27; Gromov, "Vliianie," p. 47.

49. G. A. Zhuravleva and Z. V. Sikevich, "Podgotovlennost' abiturientov i priem v vuz," in Effektivnost', ed. Leonavichius, pp. 35-39.

50. Khairullin, "Nekotorye problemy," p. 125.

51. G. I. Oparev, "Mnenie studentov vuzov ob izbrannoi spetsial'nosti," in Effektivnost', ed. Leonavichius, pp. 24-27.

52. Zhuravleva, "Nekotorye voprosy," p. 183; G. A. Zhuravleva, "Professional'noe samoopredelenie i otnoshenie k professii studencheskoi molodezhi," in Problemy, ed. Anan'ev, p. 180.

53. See, for example, Gurova and Rychkova, "Orientatsiia," pp. 152-53; A. V. Markovich, "Motivatsiia i otsenka studentami-pervokursnikami vuzov goroda L'vova budushchei professii," in Motivatsiia, ed. Leonavichius, p. 202; K. Babaitsev et al., "Govoriat budushchie spetsialisty," Ekonomicheskie nauki, no. 1 (1968): 86-88.

54. Earl Hopper, "Educational Systems and Selected Consequences of Patterns of Mobility and Non-Mobility in Industrial Societies: A Theoretical Discussion," in Readings in the Theory of Educational Systems, ed. Hopper (London: Hutchinson, 1971), pp. 305-6.

55. I. F. Obraztsov, "Nauchno-tekhnicheskaia revoliutsiia i podgotovka inzhenerov," Vestnik vysshei shkoly, no. 3 (1974): 5.

56. Rubin and Kolesnikov, Student, pp. 184-85.

57. I. Kalits, "Ob otnoshenii studentov k obshchestvennoi rabote," Kommunist Estonii, no. 4 (1968): 65-67. For similar studies, see, for example, Ruseikina, "Sotsial'nyi status," p. 43; Laptenok et al., "Kontingent Studentov," pp. 334-36.

58. S. N. Ikonnikova and V. T. Lisovskii, "Nekotorye problemy vospitaniia studencheskoi molodezhi," in Molodezh', ed. Lisovskii, p. 163.

59. A. P. Kniga, "Ob urovne obshchestvenno-politicheskoi aktivnosti studentov," in Effektivnost', ed. Leonavichius, pp. 89-90.

60. Kalits, "Ob otnoshenii," p. 66.

61. L. A. Zelenov and R. I. Nikiforov, "O tipakh orientatsii pervokursnikov," in Sichivitsa, Sotsiologiia, pp. 82-90.

62. Ruseikina, "Sotsial'nyi status," p. 42.

63. Rutkevich and Filippov, Sotsial'nye, pp. 39-47.

64. See M. Rutkevich, "Konkurs," Izvestiia, December 9, 1967; Rutkevich and Sennikova, "Sotsial'naia obuslovlennost'"; Rutkevich and Filippov, "Komplektovanie."

65. V. I. Mishin et al., "Problema sotsial'nogo sostava sovremennogo studenchestva," in Sotsiologicheskie issledovaniia, ed. Zelenkov, pp. 7-19.

NONCONFORMIST TRENDS IN THE SOVIET LITERARY PRESS: *NOVY MIR*
Alexandra Kwiatkowski

The nonconformist literary press in the socialist countries has always offered considerable attraction for anyone interested in the political, sociocultural, scientific, and economic realities in that part of the world. Traditionally the elites' reading, an "authorized" although closely watched tribune of progressives and protesters, in our time it has also become a kind of barometer of political life in the Soviet Union and in the East European countries. It has often been a precursor of a thaw, a spring, or a winter. Such is the case of Novy mir, the most prestigious Soviet literary magazine, perpetuator of the Russian tradition of tolstye zhurnaly, "spiritual country" of the Soviet nonconformist intelligentsia.

The hardening of the Soviet authorities' position toward the intellectuals in 1968, Alexander Tvardovsky's resignation in 1970 and death in 1971, have contributed to turning Western interest away from Novy mir and the officially permitted Soviet nonconformism toward open contestation and opposition. However, these marginal although more spectacular phenomena are linked to "authorized" nonconformism in the USSR.

Roy Medvedev's recent works have stimulated current interest in Soviet nonconformism. [1] Alexander Tvardovsky, and most of the contributors to Novy mir were Party Democrats before their time; this remains the trend of a part of the intelligentsia still forming a kind of bastion around Novy mir, their writings often of great interest and value.

The Party Democrats can be defined as the leftwing (progressive) current of the Communist Party of the Soviet Union, which has its ideological foundation in Marxism-Leninism. Often part of the establishment, the Party Democrats sympathize or even collaborate with the diverse opposition tendencies outside the Party, the nonconformist circles grouped around the literary journal Novy mir, the Committee of the Rights of Man, and others. They sometimes cooperate with the moderate conservatives in power, the Party majority which they consider "politically incapable" and "ideologically terrified, " and which yields

more readily to the neo-Stalinists than to the "progressives" but is
"tossed back and forth between the energetic acts which turn the Soviet
Union back toward the past and the agonizing decisions which make it
timidly progress," in Medvedev's words. One percent, or perhaps less,
of the Party, they are frequently collaborators whose competence makes
them valuable. Careful but firm, they form a political "club" acting at
various levels, sometimes within diverse organs of the state. [2]

Let us define the expression "nonconformism." In the case under
consideration, it is thought, writing, or action that rejects both unquestioning obedience to official propaganda and cultural uniformity.
In a wider sense, being a nonconformist in the USSR involves being anti-
Stalinist, critical, polemic, and sometimes challenging acts and principles of the establishment.

There is a direct or indirect link between all the elements of literary, cultural, and political nonconformism in Soviet publications and
the Communist Party's role in sociocultural and political life.

More specifically, as far as I know, Soviet publications and Novy
mir have never questioned either the dominant role of the Communist
Party of the USSR or the Soviet system—first of all, because the triple
censorship does not let through anything of the kind, but also because
the majority of Soviet intellectuals have gotten accustomed or even attached to the Party and the system. This becomes clear when one reads,
for example, a well-known speech by Grigori Svirski (a Soviet writer),
a speech that has not been published in the USSR but has been widely
diffused in the West, and known in the USSR since it was made on January 16, 1968, in Moscow in front of a crowded assembly of writers who
were Party members. "We demand freedom," Svirski said, "but not freedom outside the Party. We are the Party's flesh and blood and its interests are ours. We demand to be free from the distortions which a
clique of men impose with impunity on the Party's line." [3]

NOVY MIR AFTER ALEXANDER TVARDOVSKY

The monthly literary magazine Novy mir was founded in 1925 on the
Party's instructions. It essentially gained its reputation, however, for
its nonconformism in the 1960s, for the quality and truthfulness of the
literary works and reviews, for the originality of the economical and
political writings published in its columns while its editor-in-chief,
Alexander Tvardovsky, tirelessly fought to protect the creative freedom
of his writers from the regime's constant harassment. This liberal role
was in fact a continuation of the journal's previous role. Its "liberal"
reputation was gained as early as 1953. [4] Following this, in August
1954, the Writers' Union had already published a resolution on the
"The monthly Novy mir's errors."

Many people have interpreted Alexander Tvardovsky's resignation
in January 1970 as a sign of Novy mir's total alignment, a natural result

of a decline that began in 1968 with the Soviet authorities' crackdown
on the progressive intelligentsia after the Plenum of the Central Committee in April 1968, after the events of March 1968 in Poland, and
shortly before the armed intervention in Prague. This judgment is too
hasty and not quite exact.

At that time, in the late 1960s, Soviet authorities began to crack
down on the intelligentsia and they progressively hardened their position
in the following years. Little by little, Novy mir's staff changed hands
and Alexander Tvardovsky quit his magazine in January 1970 after an
exhausting struggle to defend his own ideals and those of a "thinking
and moral" intelligentsia that had gathered around him.

Yet in January 1968 an essay on American intellectuals by I. Kon
appeared in the magazine, an essay that Soviet nonconformist circles
unhesitatingly read as a disguised manifesto aimed at the Soviet intellectuals themselves:

> For certain people the consciousness of belonging to an elite
> begot a strong feeling of responsibility toward the people, and
> the desire to be not only the brain, but also the conscience of
> the nation. For others the same consciousness transforms it-
> self into a feeling of contempt for the masses, into snobbery
> and thirst for privileges.

One is struck by Kon's direct style and by his political thought:

> Starting with the French revolution of 1830, history has re-
> vealed that the suppression of democratic freedoms brings
> about an effect which is opposite to the hoped-for one: the
> new opposition is often much stronger than the previous
> one . . . . When there is a political crisis, repression gives
> new strength to the opponents . . . .
>   Administrative attempts to control intellectual and artistic
> life and make it conform to certain standards had but one ef-
> fect: to transform a more or less harmless intellectual op-
> position which was not really interested in the masses'
> problems (for the masses' appreciation for contemporary art
> always awakens slowly) into a political opposition much more
> dangerous from the regime's point of view. [5]

The shadow of the "ideological struggle" already hovered above
intellectual life in the Soviet Union, but Novy mir's first issues in 1968
were still quite nonconformist. The April issue published works by
Tvardovsky and the French writer of the nouveau roman, Nathalie Sar-
raute, with a postface by Lakshin. Anatolii Kuznetsov contributed a
bitter short story inspired by life in the opera, which appears as a
symbol of certain aspects of Soviet social and administrative life. [6] In
November 1968, Pravda violently reproached Novy mir with the publication of this short story "inspired by false theories" and accused it of

undermining the regime's prestige. The Party's daily newspaper called
on Novy mir on the behalf of public opinion to "at last draw the necessary conclusions from this criticism."

On the other hand, in May 1968 the magazine already reflected a
mixture of its usual nonconformism and of a certain dogmatism accepted
with reservations by a part of the staff. This was exemplified by the
unsigned editorial published in Novy mir in May 1968, after the student
demonstrations in Poland and at the time of the Czechoslovak "spring,"
but before the Warsaw Pact forces' intervention in Prague. It is quite
possible that it was both a reaction and a threat. [7] One can sense that
the authorities stood ready to clamp down as firmly as necessary on the
magazine if it resisted being brought into line.

However, Novy mir refused to conform to all the official demands.
The same May 1968 issue published writings by Vasil' Bykov, [8] Bella
Akhmadulina, Vitalii Semin, A. Mariamov, and L. Lazar'ev—editors and
contributors who have an established reputation for nonconformism.
During all the following years a more or less open resistance continued
even after Tvardovsky's resignation and death.

In the summer of 1971, on the eve of the Fifth Congress of Soviet
Writers, when an atmosphere of "ideological intransigence" and "un-
compromising struggle against bourgeois ideology" prevailed, Novy mir
quoted Bulgakov, Mandel'shtam, Babel', and Pasternak as "authentically
Soviet writers although their notion of 'socialist realism' was perhaps
not the same as is now current"—cautious but persevering resistance
to the mediocrity of official cultural views. Most certainly, this is no
longer June 1968, when Levidova had rediscovered a "Babelian tradition"
in the works of the American writer Bernard Malamud, and when Lakshin
had written a long, enthusiastic, and suggestive analysis of Bulgakov's
The Master and Margarita quoting Pushkin in an epigraph: "There can
be no criticism without love of art. Do you want to be a connoisseur of
art? Vinkelman said. Try to love the artist, look for beauty in his
work."[9] Citing also Ernest Renan on the state, justice, and police:

> When it played a perfidious role in the Golgotha torture, the
> State dealt itself a fatal blow. A legend contemptuous of
> power has triumphed and has gone round the world. The
> holders of power played a vile part in this legend. The ac-
> cused had right on his side. The judges and the police be-
> came allies against the truth. [10]

In 1968 and 1969, the magazine kept obstinately publishing writings
of already dismissed contributors like Dement'ev. [11] Polemic publications on truth, literary criticism, esthetics, and modernism were carried
on in Novy mir until 1974.

In March 1970, V. Kardin wrote:

> People who fight to uphold a new idea encounter the following
> enemies: deadly words, . . . words that oppress, words that

mask the true interests and the nullity of the people who
throw them out with self-confidence.

But who can stop thought? Hearing the familiar order:
"Do not touch the State's domain!" man answers with determination "I will," and he happily gazes at the star he just
picked from the sky. [12]

In November 1970 M. Bakhtin, reprimanded by Literaturnaia gazeta,
wrote: "Every discovery in the intellectual sphere may modify our conceptions and may even require their total revision." [13]

In 1969 and 1970 Novy mir still published many nonconformist
"verifying" works and many more or less avant-garde ones: novels and
short stories by V. Bykov, Viktor Nekrasov, I. Trifonov, E. Dorosh, A.
Tvardovsky, F. Iskander, and Albert Camus, with an epilogue by Sats,
already dismissed from the staff. However, Baklanov, Paustovskii, I.
Dombrovskii, Zalygin, and Semin, whose works were promised to readers
for 1969, did not appear that year in Novy mir. On the other hand, Lakshin, Zaks, Dement'ev, Kardin, and many of the editors and contributors
who had made a reputation for nonconformism in the 1960s continued to
appear in the magazine's columns.

Starting in 1970 a new line of polemicists begin to appear in Novy
mir, writers like I. Kon, G. Kunitsyn, E. Dobin, S. Kaidash, and the
poet E. Markin (expelled from the Writers' Union after the publication
of his poems on Solzhenitsyn). [14] The official press criticizes these
authors when they happen to succeed in cleverly circumventing censorship.

On January 27, 1971, Literaturnaia gazeta reported debates about
Novy mir and expressed reservations about many texts and contributors—
for example, about V. Bykov for his novel Sotnikov and E. Yevtushenko
for his poem "Kazan' University." [15] It sharply criticized "the Novy mir
staff's irresponsibility"; the staff took due note and proceeded to break
almost every promise made to readers in July and August 1970 about the
publications program for 1971. This was Novy mir's weakest year.

Literaturnaia gazeta expressed its displeasure and reproached
Novy mir for not following partiinost' ("Party spirit") and narodnost'
("popular spirit"), criteria peculiar to socialist realism, and for not
dedicating enough space to international politics and the ideological
struggle, the contemporary Soviet Army, or literature about the working
class and the peasantry. Novy mir complied with these requests, but
it nevertheless published official propaganda and nonconformist remarks
side by side in its columns. In a way these camouflaged progressive
and critical ideas were more insidiously effective in striking at the
authorities than were the outspoken polemic reflections of the 1960s.
Of course, it was necessary to read attentively between the lines, but
this method—a mental substitution of one situation for another one—is
deeply rooted in Russian and Soviet habits. Pushkin, Saltykov-
Shchedrin, Dostoyevsky, and Tolstoy have used it. This method is
familiar to all who write and publish in the Soviet Union and who, as

V. Turbin has said, are "specialists in text with a double meaning and
in interpreting contexts. "

In this way Novy mir devoted much attention in the 1970s to Western
dissident movements, their nature, role, and development. In this
roundabout way, and only in this roundabout way, some authors dealt
with contestation in the socialist camp. This tendency to read analogies
and comparisons with the Soviet Union into text about foreign countries
may seem an unsupported and preconceived notion. But censorship became more vigilant than ever between 1968 and 1974, and the progressive or simply "thinking and moral" intelligentsia (as Gnedin puts it)
in the socialist countries refused to remain silent and resorted to all
sorts of subterfuges to express themselves. Iurii Tomashevskii's review
of Multidimensional Voyages by Viktor Nekrasov is quite explicit on that
account:

> Wherever Nekrasov happens to be, in Italy, England, France
> or the United States, he does not sojourn as a simple tour-
> ist . . . . He is our compatriot and he observes his sur-
> roundings with our eyes. He is preoccupied by our life, by
> our destiny, and he "compares" what he sees abroad to his
> home country. [16]

In Novy mir of October 1970, E. Gnedin "plays" (the word is his)
with the reader in an essay about Western youth movements and their
problems: "I will quote, " he says, "some documents without saying
beforehand what countries they refer to. In this way the analogies and
differences will be even more striking. "[17] The Documents' impact
gradually increases:

> [From document 1] One must appeal to the ideals of the
> engineers, the intellectuals, the scientists, the teachers
> and the students . . . .
> [From document 2] We fight not only for the right . . . to
> express our opinions freely . . . the essential point is to
> abolish an oligarchic power, to struggle for democratic liber-
> ties . . . . We protest against the people who, in one way
> or another, violate the Constitution, while claiming to take
> their inspiration from it.
> [From document 3] The struggle for freedom has begun. It
> is a struggle against the bureaucratic organizations which
> deprive man of his responsibility . . . against these scien-
> tists and technicians who profit from science to increase
> their own power . . . against the pseudo-moralists who ac-
> quiesce in the injustice (of capital), and the violence exer-
> cised by the regime, and sclerosis of ideas . . . . It is also
> a struggle against mass communications that do not communi-
> cate with anybody except the professional politicians.

[From document 4] We accuse society and the personalities who direct the state, and the business and science
world of having but one aim: to preserve their own positions . . . . Society has betrayed its noble traditions. The
Constitution guarantees freedom of speech and of assembly,
but the smallest opposition is systematically, sometimes
violently stamped out. Our society is said to be democratic
and representative, but the political apparatus makes decisions on its own authority, disregarding the nation's opinion . . . . The older generation is essentially preoccupied
with its material well-being and thus it has forgotten ethical
values; it swears loyalty to ideals and unprotestingly accepts
the surrounding hypocrisy. It fears change and does not keep
its way of life under control any more. [18]

It is tempting to play the game with Gnedin and to recognize in
these documents the dissidents' anger—against incompetence; against
dogmatism; against the inefficiency of the mass communications media
and their subjugation to the regime; against the sham of elections and
the arbitrariness of the regime's decisions; against the systematic opposition to progress and the disproportionately high standard of living
of some officials.

To conclude, let us quote an extract from document 5: "If only it
were possible to discuss political problems without being afraid!," a
young Italian says. [19]

In January 1970, while Zhurnalist was writing that the majority of
Soviet writers are "Soldiers on the front line of ideological combat and
under the Party's direction," S. Kaidash was quoting Herzen in Novy
mir: "For the people deprived of political freedom, literature is the only
tribune from which the cry of their conscience and their opposition
echoes."[20] G. Kunitsyn, reprimanded by Literaturnaia gazeta on January
27, 1971, developed the same quotation more extensively in Novy mir
in November 1970. [21] Then, after a year-long silence, other people
spoke out in Novy mir: In July 1972 Alexander Ianov went beyond literary criticism, writing that the literary hero reflects a society that entitles or fails to entitle the citizen to take an original part in state
affairs, and that the heroes' protest in the 1960s was expressed in a
spontaneous and rash way, whereas the heroes in the 1970s propose an
alternative program. [22] One again meets this "positivism" in Novy mir
in O. Moroz's article entitled "Galilea's Struggle" in April 1973: Is it
worth defending the truth against unprincipled politicians? Isn't it
worth making some clever compromises, while putting together arguments and grouping supporters for truth and morality? The Party Democrats' position as defined by Roy Medvedev appears quite similar.

NOVY MIR ON THE EVE OF ITS FIFTIETH ANNIVERSARY

Throughout 1973 and 1974, Novy mir continued to publish truthful
and realistic novels, short stories, essays, and reviews; arguments for
morality (this leitmotiv unites the different currents in the Soviet dissident movement); and arguments for humanism and freedom of creation.
Interesting and good text appeared by V. Tendriakov, F. Abramov, I.
Trifonov, L. Lazar'ev, V. Latyshev, I. Kon, V. Kataev, F. Iskander, B.
Mozhaev, A. Ianov, A. Kurgatnikov and V. Bubnis, V. Kardin, I. Nagibin, V. Kovskii, V. Turbin, and the Sinologist A. Zhelokhovtsev. [23] The
excellent nonconformist writers F. Abramov and B. Mozhaev, for example, limited themselves to the publication of high-quality stories inspired by country life in the 1950s and 1960s; B. Mozhaev apologizes
for this in his foreword and modestly entitles his writings "Old Stories."
Nevertheless, these texts are of great interest and actuality.
Let us cite F. Abramov in January 1973:

"Ivan Dimitrievich why do they say there are saboteurs
in the country?"
"Saboteurs?"
"Yes, academicians, they say, who wanted to sabotage
the Russian language."
"To sabotage the Russian language," marveled Arkadii
Iakovlev. "What do you mean?"
"Yes, yes," Ignatii Baev nodded in approval.
"I've heard that, too, Iosif Visarionovich himself lec-
tured them. In the newspaper Pravda . . . ."
"There you are!" The old peasant gave a sigh. "Last
year cosmopolitans sold us to foreign states, this year it's
the academicians!"[24]

A dialogue by B. Mozhaev in April 1974:

The better we live, the more we deviate.
"Deviate from what?" I asked.
"Well, deviate from the Party line of course!"[25]

Also:

I remember a lecture at the club, Evsei Petrovich was sit-
ting in the first row . . . and he asked a question:
"Could you tell us what things are like in Indonesia?"
"What things?" the lecturer asked.
"Well, do they have order there? I mean, don't they
need us to help?"[26]

In August 1973, Novy mir published a satirical short story, "The Hurricane," by Khosrow Shakhani, which appears as a tragicomic reflection on the official campaign against dissidents and nonconformists in the Soviet Union, and on the trial of Yakir and Krasin. Novy mir may claim to have acted quite innocently: The story's author is Iranian, and the censor's visa was accorded to that issue of Novy mir on August 3, when only the best-informed circles knew what the date, the development, and the outcome of the trial would be. Novy mir actually is well informed, but it can on occasion pretend the contrary. This careful attitude spared the staff a lot of pressures and sanctions recently. However, contributors to the magazine did not react passively to the upcoming tempest against the truth of facts and against the human rights Novy mir has not ceased to defend.

It is the very first time that Novy mir has published a text (even a foreign one) about a trial of opinion. The short story deserves being quoted in extenso, and it actually was cited in extenso by the Polish Catholic newspaper Tygodnik powszechny:[27]

I shall quote only the last few paragraphs:

> Next, the Governor dictated the Court's verdict to the clerk: Insofar as the accused confessed before witnesses that his letter written on such and such date aimed at slandering the town's true benefactors before the highest authorities, in application of paragraph b of the twelfth item of section 247966 of the law on penal responsibility for casting hateful aspersions, but taking into consideration the accused's sincere repentance, and applying maximum clemency to his case, the Court has decided that during six months, three times a day, for one hour each time, the accused will stand in the market square and shout the slogan: "Down with traitors and agents in our enemies' pay!"
>
> I was in deepest despair. A lump in my throat, I could neither speak, nor cry. The jurymen left the court and I followed them, accompanied by a guard.
>
> The street was swept by such a sandstorm that we lost sight of each other. The wind blew so strongly that we stopped moving, closing our eyes and not daring to look around us. I felt like shouting: "Excellency! High Court! If this is not a hurricane, then what is it?" But the hurricane did not even let us open our mouths, still less express ourselves. All the doors were closed. The streets were deserted. The wind was howling like a hungry wolf and it was blowing everything away.[28]

In the January 1974 issue of Novy mir appears a review of a book dedicated to psychiatry. At a moment when more and more numerous appeals were being made to scientists all over the world, as well as

more and more numerous protests inside the Soviet Union against the
confinement of some intellectuals in KGB psychiatric hospitals, and
against sentences to labor camp or banishment, the reader's attention
is drawn to a verse by Pushkin:

> God save me from madness. I would prefer the stick and the
> scrip, I would prefer labor and hunger. [29]

Once again turning to a subject of current interest, the July 1974
issue of the journal contains a sort of polemic on the rights of man and
their importance in the Geneva Conference. L. Leont'ev, in "The Trojan
Horse of Anticommunism," violently denounces the theory of convergence
(of which Andrei Sakharov is the spokesman in the USSR) and writes:
"The enemies of peace are launching a so-called campaign 'in favor of
the rights of man,' commenting backhandedly on the freedom to exchange ideas, in fact, trying to impose their ideas on us, they are doing
everything to make more difficult the normalization of relations between
states with different social systems."[30] To this L. Lazar'ev (who had
belonged to Tvardovsky's team) replies, perhaps without wanting to:
"I would like you to know people who repeat the same thing, independently of currents, fashions and campaigns: one must think about man-
kind. It is easy to make fun of them by talking about the present
situation, but it is difficult to lift oneself up to the level of their
thought."[31]

Novy mir's program for 1975 was published in August 1974; it looked
promising. Notably, the magazine was scheduled to publish Franz Kaf-
ka's The Castle. One can also notice in this publication program the
return, begun in 1974, of an important part of Tvardovsky's team (F.
Abramov, B. Mozhaev, V. Semin, I. Dombrovskii, V. Tendriakov).

However, Novy mir's fiftieth anniversary (1925-75) has been accompanied by a change in leadership, and apparently in tendency. The
new editor-in-chief, the poet Sergei Narovchatov, is secretary of the
Directing Committee of the Union of Writers of the USSR and also leads
the Moscow section of the Union and is a deputy of the Supreme Soviet
of the Russian Federation. He presents the image of a conservative.
Upon his return from Italy in March 1968, in his poem "Ambassador to
Florence," published at that time in Novy mir, Narovchatov wrote:

> Here [in Moscow] we don't need
> God to protect us
> From the clever games of the spirit;
> It's severe masters we need,
> Masters who know how to be hard. [32]

He also upheld the official theses on the role of the intelligentsia and
declared in March 1970, at the Third Congress of Writers of the USSR:
"Blok destroyed the blind belief of the intellectuals that their role was

to oppose every regime and every society. 'Arrogant professional politicians,' in these terms full of scorn he stigmatized their desire to impose their opinions and conjectures on the victorious people."[33]

In the last issues of 1974, Novy mir, under the editorship of S.
Narovchatov, did not publish any of the nonconformist writers of Tvardovsky's former team. The only remaining members of Tvardovsky's staff
are S. Aitmatov, R. Gamzatov, A. Kulechov, and K. Fedin. Furthermore,
Vladimir Bogomolov's spy story, "August 1944" (otherwise not without
interest), which suggests that the Polish noncommunist resistance col-
laborated with the German occupants and with Vlasov's "bands," and
whose publication the news agency TASS officially announced, is a hard
blow to the hopes of the former Novy mir team, for whom the truth of
facts had become the principal literary demand in the Soviet Union.[34]

Until the present months, which will need very careful study, nonconformism was expressed in Novy mir, even if this report suggests
how difficult it was to express it. Its spokesmen, thorough chameleons,
disguised their writings to escape the censors' attention. But in doing
so, did they not risk escaping the attention of many readers, too? Yet
the magazine's circulation did temporarily increase slightly (175,000
copies) in the Soviet Union, and one cannot help wondering if certain
progressive circles inside the power structure did not protect Novy mir
as A. Tvardovsky, who nowadays appears as a Party Democrat before
his time, did for decades.

Intellectual, literary, and artistic activities in the Soviet Union
form a complex sector animated by different currents. As the Party apparatus itself is composed of representatives of different tendencies
(moderate conservatives, Party Democrats, neo-Stalinist chauvinists),
"liberal" and "conservative" phases follow one another and modify the
balance of power.

The nonconformist phenomenon is visible in Novy mir from 1968 to
1974—the period treated in this essay—although many pressures and
vexations affect the nonconformist spokesmen. They emanate from the
highest Soviet Communist Party authorities, as well as from the "orthodox" and neo-Stalinist circles still powerful inside Soviet cultural and
intellectual life.

Novy mir, and occasionally other literary magazines, often chooses
specific themes to manifest nonconformism (anti-Stalinism, the fight
for truth, for morality, and for legality). One realizes as one goes along,
however, that it is really impossible to compartmentalize these themes.
One must also compare Novy mir and Oktiabr' to discern how, to what
extent, and in which domains nonconformism appears.

Generally speaking, until 1968, Novy mir set forth problems inher-
ent in the USSR and Soviet society. Since 1968 it has been more interested in world political, cultural, and economic life and in the general
problems of society, but through them it still attempts to reveal (if not

to solve) its country's specific preoccupations. Allusions to history, analogies to other countries, quotations, nuances, and innuendoes are part of what in a word is known as nonconformism. However, it is not always easy for the reader—or the censor—to tell where there is a protest cleverly disguised in a text using the official propaganda leitmotiv to return the sting against the Soviet system's imperfections, and where there is a text simply obeying the regime's instructions.

The slogan for the ideological struggle confirmed by the Twenty-fourth Party Congress and by the Fifth Writers' Congress has struck a hard blow to nonconformism. (In 1971, Novy mir's content was quite mediocre, and this might again be the case in 1975.) Nevertheless, one cannot say that there is a return to "Stalinism." The late Arkadii Belnikov, a onetime member of the Union of Soviet Writers, stated that "there are, in fact, no insurmountable barriers and nothing which cannot be attempted in post-Stalin literature. Even today, however, no matter how black the picture is painted, if the censor makes some radical change in a work, one has to blame both the censor and the author who permits this to happen."[35] His views agree with those of Solzhenitsyn and Siniavsky.[36] In fact, a part of the intelligentsia has refined its legitimate inclination for public and private liberties, and its demands and verbal violence have risen in intensity.

What then is Novy mir's role?

1. It could be a kind of lure to identify and perhaps to neutralize the nonconformist intellectuals who group themselves around Novy mir.

2. It could have been an "authorized" institution in literary and sociocultural life, which afforded a maximum of concessions to the Soviet elite, concessions tolerated by Leonid Brezhnev's staff, and perhaps obtained by the "democrats" inside the Party, now more than ever obliged to remain careful and anonymous.

In either case, Novy mir has been until now, and in the long run will probably remain, a "spiritual fatherland" for some Soviet intellectuals. But if it is not always read and understood by a wide public, one can question the impact of the tolstyi zhurnal's traditional missionary role of "the tribune from which echoes the cry of the intellectual and popular conscience and opposition." The true impact of Novy mir deserves to be studied by means of a public opinion poll impossible to effect in satisfactory conditions. (This author has attempted to contact past and present contributors to Novy mir living in the Soviet Union and elsewhere; their responses will be part of a doctoral thesis.) However, the echoes that the magazine inspires, and the place it is accorded in power circles, in the Soviet press, in the press of other socialist countries, and in the Western mass media, reflect the large scale of this impact—which, however, does not reach the masses. Issues of Novy mir are bought up within a few hours of publication, and it should be noted that the literary and political turning point announced under Sergei Narovchatov's leadership has been accompanied by a drop in the magazine's circulation, which fell from 175, 000 to 165, 000 and then to 160, 000 in three months, but rose to 175, 000 again in 1975.

The issues of Novy mir's fifty-first year are awaited with curiosity and some worry. If Narovchatov had to be (or to appear) "hard" to accede to Novy mir's editorship, in the long term will he have to be moderate or even liberal to exercise it?

NOTES

1. Roy Medvedev, Le Stalinisme (Paris: Le Seuil, 1972) and De la democratie socialiste (Paris: Grasset, 1972); Zhores Medvedev, Dix ans dans la vie de Soljenitsyne (Paris: Grasset, 1974).

2. R. Medvedev, De la democratie socialiste; Vladimir Gedilaghine, Les contestataires en U.R.S.S. (Paris: Casterman, 1974); Alexandra Kwiatkowski, "La Democracia Socialista," Revista Espanola de la Opinion Publica, no. 31 (1973): 470-75.

3. Le Monde, April 28-29, 1968, p. 3.

4. V. Pomerantsev, "Ob iskrennosti v literature," Novy mir 29, no. 12 (1953): 218-45.

5. I. Kon, "Razmyshleniia ob amerikanskoi intelligentsii," Novy mir 44, no. 1 (1968): 176, 190.

6. Anatolii Kuznetsov, "Artist mimansa," Novy mir 44, no. 4 (1968): 58-71.

7. "Osnovopolozhnik nauchnogo kommunizma," Novy mir 44, no. 5 (1968): 3-7.

8. Vasil' Bykov, "Ataka s khodu," Novy mir 44, no. 5 (1968): 10-71.

9. V. Lakshin, "Roman M. Bulgakova 'Master i Margarita,'" Novy mir 44, no. 6 (1968): 284.

10. Ibid., p. 296.

11. Aleksandr Dement'ev, "Roman o Maiakovskom," Novy mir 44, no. 6 (1968): 323-28; "Kniga o sovetskoi estetike," Novy mir 44, no. 7 (1968): 253-58; "O traditsiiakh i narodnosti," Novy mir 45, no. 4 (1969): 215-35; "Simvol very poeta," Novy mir 45, no. 9 (1969): 239-43.

12. V. Kardin, "Smeiat'sia, pravo, ne greshno . . . ," Novy mir 46, no. 3 (1970): 249.

13. M. Bakhtin, "Smelee pol'zovat'sia vozmozhnostiami," Novy mir 46, no. 11 (1970): 240.

14. Evgenii Markin, "Belyi baken," Novy mir 47, no. 10 (1971): 96-98.

15. Vasil' Bykov, "Sotnikov," Novy mir 46, no. 5 (1970): 65-161; and Evg [enii] Evtuskhenko, "Kazanskii universitet," Novy mir 46, no. 4 (1970): 46-89.

16. Iurii Tomashevskii, Review of Viktor Nekrasov, Puteshestviia v raznykh izmereniiakh, Novy mir 44, no. 1 (1968): 278.

17. E. Gnedin, "Utrachennye illiuzii i obretennye nadezhdy," Novy mir 46, no. 10 (1970): 180.

18. Ibid., pp. 180-81.

19. Ibid., p. 181.

20. S. Kaidash, "V. Dal' i ego biograf," Novy mir 46, no. 1 (1970): 247.

21. G. Kunitsyn, "Spetsifika iskusstva," Novy mir 46, no. 10 (1970): 241.

22. Aleksandr Ianov, "Dvizhenie molodogo geroia," Novy mir 48, no. 7 (1972): 233.

23. V. Tendriakov, "Vesennie perevertyshi," Novy mir 49, no. 1 (1973): pp. 118-71; Fedor Abramov, "Puti-pereput'ia," no. 1, pp. 3-114, and no. 2, pp. 5-58, and "Aledsandr Iashin, poet i prozaik," no. 4, pp. 249-52; Iurii Trifonov, "Neterpenie," no. 3, pp. 44-116, no. 4, pp. 35-112, no. 5, pp. 8-90; V. Latyshev, "'Pod uglom volnuiushchikh voprosov . . . ,'" no. 6, pp. 251-53; I Kon, "Druzhba," no. 7, pp. 165-83; Valentin Kataev, "Fialka," no. 8, pp. 74-95; Fazil' Iskander, "Sandro iz Chegema," no. 8, pp. 152-88, no. 9, pp. 70-104, no. 10, pp. 100-32, and no. 11, pp. 71-125; Boris Mozhaev, "Den' bez kontsa i bez kraia," no. 9, 11. 19-66; Iurii Nagibin, "Dialog s drugorn," no. 9, pp. 269-71.

Mozhaev, "Starye istorii," Novy mir 50, no. 4 (1974): 61-95; Ianov, "Razumnoe, dobroe, vechnoe . . . ," no. 8, pp. 268-71; Aleksandr Kurgatnikov, "S utra do vechera," no. 1, pp. 22-34; Vitantas Bubnis, "Tri dnia v avguste," no. 1, pp. 17-65, and no. 2, pp. 52-141; V. Kardin, "O lebediakh i 'lebedushkakh,'" no. 2, pp. 264-68; Vadim Kovskii, "'Bud' zaodno s geniem . . . ,'" no. 1, pp. 232-49; V. Turbin, "Taina ili sekret?" no. 1, pp. 277-80; A. Zhelokhovtsev, "'Doloi teoriiu vdokhnovleniia!'," no. 4, pp. 237-46, and "Pogonia za Konfutsiem," no. 7, pp. 250-55.

24. Abramov, "Puti-pereput'ia," Novy mir 49, no. 1 (1973): 8.

25. Mozhaev, "Starye istorii," Novy mir 50, no. 4 (1974): 62.

26. Ibid., p. 79.

27. Chosrou Szachani, "Huragan," Tygodnik powszechny, October 21, 1973, p. 1.

28. Khosrou Shakhani, "Uragan," Novy mir 49, no. 8 (1973): 40.

29. Turbin, "Taina ili sekret," p. 278.

30. L. Leont'ev, "Troianskii kon' antikommunizma," Novy mir 50, no. 7 (1974): 275-80.

31. L. Lazar'ev, "Eto pechatalos' v gazeta," Novy mir 50, no. 7 (1974): 270-75.

32. S. Narovchatov, "Russkii posol vo Florentsii," Novy mir 44, no. 3 (1968): 135.

33. Tretii s''ezd pisatelei RSFSR (Moscow: Sovetskaia Rossiia, 1972), p. 242.

34. Vladimir Bogomolov, "V avguste 1944 . . . ," Novy mir 50, no. 10 (1974): 3-109, no. 11, pp. 5-95, and no. 12, pp. 161-232.

35. Martin Dewhirst and Robert Farrell, eds., The Soviet Censorship (Metuchen, N.J.,: Scarecrow Press, 1973), p. 10.

36. Pierre Daix, Ce que je sais de Soljenitsyne (Paris: Le Seuil, 1973), and Abram Tertz (Andrei Siniavskii), "Literaturnyi protsess v Rossii," Kontinent, no. 1 (1974): 143-90.

5

THE ROLE AND EVOLUTION
OF PRESS AGENCIES IN
THE SOCIALIST COUNTRIES
Theodore E. Kruglak

This discussion of the role and evolution of press agencies in the socialist countries seeks to trace the relationships between the national and international news agencies that formed the international news cartel of the nineteenth century, the influence of the telegraph upon the international news flow, and the emergence of the press agencies in the European socialist countries. "Press" and "news" are used interchangeably in this study. "News agency" is the preferred term for contemporary agencies since their service is not limited to the press but includes radio and television as well.

The historical aspects of the national agencies are divided into the following sections: (1) Relations with the international news cartel; (2) the period between World War I and World War II; (3) the emergence of TASS (Telegrafnoe Agentstvo Sovetskogo Soiuza—the Telegraphic Agency of the Soviet Union), and (4) the post-World War II developments.

For the purpose of this essay, the writer has defined a national news agency as a news-gathering and distribution organization concentrating its major resources within its home country and relying to a great extent upon agreements with other national and international news agencies for foreign news.

An international agency, on the other hand, is primarily concerned with gathering news throughout the world and distributing it through national agencies or directly to the news media or individual clients in foreign countries.

These definitions are valid in describing the news agencies of the nineteenth century, but there has been a major shift since 1950 and the lines of demarcation have become blurred. International agencies frequently serve as national agencies within their own countries, for example, Associated Press and United Press International in the United

This essay was previously published in Gazette 21, no. 1 (Amsterdam, 1975): 1-18 and is reprinted with permission.

States, TASS in the Soviet Union, and Agence France-Presse in France. On the other hand, a number of national agencies have correspondents throughout the world and distribute their news to individual news media and agencies abroad.

This study is confined to the news agencies of the European socialist countries, where there is a common historical thread that is lacking in China, Cuba, or Korea.

THE ERA OF THE INTERNATIONAL NEWS CARTEL

News agency development in Europe may be traced to the concept of spheres of influence and the economic expansion of the nineteenth century, and the necessity for fast reliable information concerning stock market developments in Berlin, Frankfurt, Hamburg, London, Paris, Amsterdam, and other financial and trade centers.

Political considerations may have been combined with economics, the new nationalism, and the free trade movement, as was the case in the fourteenth century when the House of Fugger provided relatively rapid news service from a worldwide network of correspondents.

Today's news agencies spring directly from the financial service of Charles Havas, an expatriate Hungarian who settled in Paris and started his venture in the second decade of the nineteenth century. Havas organized a network of correspondents throughout Europe and from Paris supplied information to private individuals, diplomats, traders, and financiers.

The early transmissions had to rely for speed upon the ingenuity of the correspondents. In this pre-telegraph period Havas's agents took advantage of express carriages, dispatch riders, pigeons, and semaphores to hasten the flow of financial data from the farflung reaches of Europe to Paris, where the material was translated by a staff of bilingual employees for delivery to the financial news centers. Havas soon encountered competition from two of his former employees who had served as translators. Julius Reuter, a native of the Free State of Hesse, and Bernard Wolff, a Prussian, achieved success from their respective bases in London and Berlin. [1]

The competition increased as the telegraph spread throughout Europe. The telegraph was considered, at least in continental Europe, a state monopoly primarily for the transmission of diplomatic messages— although by 1848 the telegraph had been opened to the general public. At first, lines did not go beyond national frontiers and telegrams had to be carried by hand across boundary lines to the nearest terminal to continue the journey.

When Prussia attempted to establish telegraph links with localities near its national frontiers in 1848, it was obliged to negotiate fifteen separate conventions with the German states to obtain transit rights. The first international telegraph convention was concluded between

Prussia and Austria on October 3, 1849. It concerned the establishment and use of electromagnetic telegraphs for the exchange of state messages. [2]

The period between 1849 and 1864 could very well be called a conventional age, for in this fifteen-year span more than 30 individual conventions were signed.

The first agreement between Havas, Reuter, and Wolff occurred in 1856; it covered the exchange of financial information, primarily stock quotations and market prices.

Despite this early agreement, the one world of the international news cartel did not arrive without a struggle. Power politics interfered. Wolff's agency, as the chosen communication instrument of Prussian expansion, could not stand by while Reuter, following the British flag, was flirting with the opponents of German unification.

Reuter obtained a toehold in Germany through a concession from the king of Hanover to construct a cable linking England with Hamburg, Bremen, and Hanover, centers of the old Hanseatic League that were actively opposed to Bismarck's integration aims. When Hanover was annexed to Prussia in 1866, the front of the struggle to control the communication of information shifted to the Lowlands. Reuter and Havas combined forces to oppose Wolff.

The struggle between France and Prussia on the political and military plane was foreshadowed by the tactical moves of Havas to forestall Wolff's attempt to supply the Belgian and Dutch press with Prussian-oriented news. Reuter and Havas set up a joint office in Brussels out of which grew subagencies at Antwerp, Ghent, and Bruges. Reuter moved into Amsterdam. [3]

The only major news agency not in either camp was the K. K. Telegraphen-Korrespondenz Bureau (KKTK) in Vienna. The official agency of the Austro-Hungarian Empire was a power of sorts—as long as it reflected the prestige of the Osterreich. It took advantage of the official telegraph lines running from Vienna through Russia into the Scandinavian countries to build a small news empire of its own. Through exchange agreements with the Russian news agency and Ritzaus of Denmark, it was, in a sense, a competitor to Wolff and Reuter. But no one appeared to be concerned. [4]

It was the Vienna-Copenhagen link that permitted the last great reporting achievement of the independent agencies of the nineteenth century to be accomplished. The KKTK correspondent pierced the Prussian lines to flash the details of the Battle of Custozza in 1866 and the defeat of Prussia's ally, Italy, by the Austrians. The feat of the KKTK editors was accomplished by transmitting the news via St. Petersburg to Copenhagen, reaching the Russian and Scandinavian press a good 24 hours ahead of the Wolff report. [5]

The news titans' conflict during this period was disastrous to the agencies of the little countries of Europe. On one side were Reuter and Havas with little or no official government support. Opposed to them

was the Wolff agency, reorganized through an influx of capital from
Berlin bankers, arranged by the king of Prussia. Under its new name,
the Continental Telegraph Company, it became the press agency of the
German unification movement. It was the recipient of preferred treatment by the Prussian telegraph system, which stretched its definition
of "official correspondence" to enable Wolff to gain priority (and lower
costs) over the Reuter messages, which were treated as "private" and
permitted to pile up in transmitting centers. [6]

The national agencies had little freedom of movement during the
news war. Some, like Ritzaus, the Danish agency, asserted their independence temporarily and withstood German and British attempts to
buy them out; others, like the Amsterdam News Agency, sold out to
Reuter; others, like Stefani in Italy, were in the Havas camp; still
others, like the Russian Telegraphic Agency, were not worth fighting
over at the time. Regardless of their allegiance during the internecine
warfare, the national agencies found themselves pawns of international
news politics. When the contest resolved itself into a stalemate, a
negotiated peace ensued among the proprietors of Reuters, Havas, and
Wolff. [7]

The news treaty of 1870 provided for a division of the world into a
number of zones, in each of which one of the agencies had an exclusive
right to gather and distribute news. It also recognized for the first time
the existence of the United States as a news territory and included the
Associated Press of New York as a junior partner. The zones were as
follows:

Havas: France, Switzerland, Italy, Spain, Portugal, Egypt (shared
    with Reuters), Central and South America.
Reuters: The British Empire, Egypt (shared with Havas), Turkey,
    the Far East.
Wolff: Germany, Austria, the Netherlands, Scandinavia, Russia,
    and the Balkans. (Wolff was also to pay the other two agencies
    a considerable compensatory indemnity.)
AP, New York: The territory of the United States. [8]

The international news cartel existed as a worldwide monopoly for
almost 50 years with minor changes, such as substitution of the Associated Press of Illinois for the Associated Press of New York (the Associated Press of Illinois developed into today's Associated Press). It
was not until World War I that the structure began to crumble under the
onslaughts of American agencies in Latin America and the Far East, and
Reuter's invasion of Wolff's Balkan zone.

It may be said that the cartel fell apart when faced with the new
priorities of American economic and political policies, the geographical
divisions created at Versailles, the Russian revolution, and the emergence of new nations that did not recognize the zones of influence
created in 1870.

THE EMERGENCE OF THE SOCIALIST MODEL

The allocation of the Russian and Balkan areas to Wolff under the 1870 news treaty is interesting in the light of the emergence of the socialist countries and their news agencies following World War II. The immediate impact, however, was to remove the Russian news agency from the domination of Austro-Hungarian news sources. From 1870 until 1914 the Russian national news agencies had love-hate relationships with Wolff. At first, the shift in contracts did not bother the Russian government unduly. The flow of news within Russia was practically non-existent due to harsh censorship regulations, and the Foreign Ministry cared little about what reached the controlled agency. After all, there was a natural affinity between Russia and Germany, buttressed later by the secret Russo-German treaty of 1887 under which Russia and Germany promised, if either became involved with a third great power, to maintain a benevolent neutrality.

But the political honeymoon did not last. Five years after Bismarck was dropped by William II, the German Foreign Office declined to renew the treaty on the ground of incompatibility with the terms of its alliance with Austria and Italy.

Although Germany renounced the defense treaty, through Wolff it maintained its news hold on the Russian Empire, a stricture that now became onerous. The Russian Telegraph Agency, which had been reorganized in 1893 with a substantial subsidy from the Ministry of Foreign Affairs, was powerless to adapt its news sources to the changing alliances. Under the cartel agreements, the Russian agency could do business only with Wolff. It mattered not that France and Russia were now bound by a secret treaty to a common defense against Germany and its allies, or that heavy French investments were propping up the tsarist regime and that speedy transmission of economic news from Paris was essential to the Russian bankers. The Russian Telegraph Agency's link to the world—with full consent of Havas, now a government-subsidized agency—was solely through Wolff

Of course, there was nothing to prevent the Russian Telegraph Agency from setting up its own international service if it was prepared to station correspondents in the chief news centers and to battle the national news agencies in each country, including those of its nation's allies, France and England. [9]

There were voices protesting the Wolff ties. Count Witte, on February 28, 1902, wrote to the minister of internal affairs, giving reasons for his desire to establish a competing news agency:

Information of news concerning Russia abroad, and at the same time, the reception of news from abroad, is concentrated, at the present time, mainly in the hands of the Russian Telegraph Agency. This institution, having few of its own

representatives abroad, is connected by agreements with the
German Wolff agency, by which it receives almost all of its
news. Thus telegraph releases from abroad come under the
control and censorship of the Wolff agency, which uses this
censorship from the point of view of German interests; in
connection with incidents within the ministry under direction,
there are instances known to me wherein this agency refused
to transmit telegrams highly important to us, which, in its
opinion did not coincide with German interests. [10]

Pal'gunov, former director of TASS, described the situation in these
terms:

> General opinion in this country rather sharply expressed
> dissatisfaction with the Russian Telegraph Agency and its
> slavish dependence upon the German Wolff agency; this de-
> pendence frequently disturbed even the activities of the
> government apparatus. The government, forced to deal with
> this dissatisfaction, announced in a report from the minister
> of internal affairs to the Tsar in 1904 that: "The Russian
> Telegraph Agency is not able either to acquire equality in
> the union of foreign telegraph agencies and act with them
> toward an agreement concerning the distribution of informa-
> tion, or obtain direct relationships with the foreign press."[11]

Tsar Nicholas II reacted to the report by decreeing the creation of
a new agency absorbing the Russian Telegraph Agency. His decree of
July 21, 1904, established the St. Petersburg Telegraph Agency, under
the control of the Ministry of Finance and subsidized by it. The general
direction of the agency was entrusted to a council of three directors
representing the Ministry of Finance, the Ministry of Internal Affairs,
and the Ministry of Foreign Affairs. The only drawback was the unchanged relationship with Wolff. Neither the tsar nor the resources of
the ministries were able to alter the terms of the international cartel
agreement. Russia still was German news territory.
    Although there were grumblings among the Witte wing of the govern-
ment at this knuckling under to the Prussian agency, others saw it in a
different light. The international situation had changed to the extent
that Russo-German relations were amicable once more; further, the
Japanese War had brought Associated Press and other correspondents
into St. Petersburg and they were to remain throughout the rest of the
tsarist regime; finally, the temporary granting of freedom to the Russian
press, and the subsequent independent and anti-government correspondence of Russian exiles, indicated that it would be far better to receive
world news through one controllable source. With the reinstitution of
censorship, it was possible to screen the Wolff reports before the St.
Petersburg Telegraph Agency forwarded the dispatches to its subscribers.

One additional change was made in the agency's status: In 1909 the St.
Petersburg agency was attached directly to the Council of Ministers—a
move later copied by the Bolsheviks with the founding of their news
agency.

World War I changed the news habits of the St. Petersburg agency
as well as its name. The Russification of St. Petersburg to Petrograd
meant no alteration in the agency's structure, but the war with Germany
created the first crack in the foundation of the international news cartel.
The cartel, which had withstood the pressures of the Franco-German
War of 1870, did not emerge unscathed from World War I. Reuters, in
behalf of the British Ministry of Information, distributed news wherever
there was a taker. Havas, which had always given its news a Gallic
slant, became more of a government mouthpiece than ever. Together,
these agencies made a concerted attack on the Wolff clients, concluding
agreements with many of them—including the Petrograd Telegraph Agency. [12]

The Petrograd Telegraph Agency continued to function as a government news agency throughout the war. There are several versions of
what happened to it during the revolution. According to one report:

> Among the important buildings it was necessary to seize from
> the bourgeoisie was that of the PTA—the Petrograd Telegraphic
> Agency. It was captured on 26 October, 1917, at nine o'clock
> in the evening by a unit of Baltic sailors . . . . But when the
> first Soviet "journalists" came to the building—the journalists
> being several sailors—they were welcomed by a lone porter
> who said with surprise: "You're coming to us? But the officials
> have gone away." Not only had they gone away but took with
> them money and typewriters. [13]

Another version was given to this writer by a former editor of PTA,
who said that most of the agency editors remained on the job until it
became obvious that they were being retained only until the Bolsheviks
could train their own editors to handle the complicated task of transmitting and receiving telegrams from abroad. Evidently the last of the pre-
revolution editors were eliminated in the Lenin purges of the 1920s. [14]
Lenin did not overlook the political importance of maintaining the
Petrograd agency as a window on the world, and he retained the agreement made with Reuters during the war. As early as December 1917 Lenin
added his signature to those of Count Witte, P. A. Stolypin, and Tsar
Nicholas II on the list of names that had appeared on the agency's char-
ter in the past. He even carried over the agency's legal identification
with the tsarist Council of Ministers by attaching it to the Council of
People's Commissars of the Russian Federated Socialist Republic. [15]
The Petrograd Telegraph Agency did not retain its monopoly long.
It may be that the Bolsheviks distrusted the remaining pre-revolution
editors. Pal'gunov describes the change as follows: "Parallel with the

Petrograd Telegraph Agency existed the Press Bureau of the All-Russian Central Executive Committee of Workers, Peasants and Soldiers Deputies."[16]

The new agency transmitted communiques and decrees to newspapers in the communist area and attempted to perform a similar function internationally by using a then infant medium—radio—to bypass capitalist newspaper correspondents and editors abroad who were not using the reports of the Petrograd Telegraph Agency but preferred the sensational dispatches from Riga, Vienna, and Berlin.

The two Soviet agencies were in conflict, with neither serving as a workable instrument of international communication. To bring a semblance of order out of chaos, Lenin merged the agencies in the spring of 1918 under the name, Russian Telegraph Agency, or ROSTA. The newly incorporated agency assumed the propaganda functions of the Petrograd Telegraph Agency. Within the agency there was a section called AGIT-ROSTA, which issued bulletins to Party workers. Its contribution to the propaganda cause was a modest one; it concentrated on the immediate task of creating and distributing slogans to combat army desertions, counterrevolutionaries, hoarders, and typhus-bearing lice.[17]

AGIT-ROSTA outlived its usefulness within the news agency quickly. The task of organizing and training agitators and propagandists was scarcely one for which the agency was equipped. This duty was reassigned to the professionally trained Communist Party AGIT-COLLECTIVE, which operated independently.[18]

Stripped of its propaganda and agitation functions, ROSTA began to resemble a Western news agency.

SOCIALIST NEWS AGENCIES BETWEEN THE WARS

TASS, in a way, owed its creation to the Tenth All-Russian Congress of Soviets. Stalin introduced a resolution proposing the creation of a Union of Soviet Socialist Republics. A commission of delegates drew up a treaty of union among the Soviet socialist republics of Russia, Belorussia, Ukraine, and Transcaucasia. The Tenth Congress of the RSFSR became the First Congress of the USSR. A constitution was ratified in 1925, creating, with the addition of Uzbekistan and Turkmenistan, a union of six republics.[19]

As a consequence of this move, ROSTA, the national agency of the RSFSR, was comparable with BELTA, the Belorussian national agency, TURKMENTAG, the Turkmen national agency, and RATAU, the Ukrainian national agency. A logical assumption, in the light of those times, is that Russia did not wish to downgrade the importance and offend the national pride of the other republics by giving ROSTA, a national agency, sole control of international news. The simplest solution was to return ROSTA to the status it had in 1918-national agency of the RSFSR. The myth of equality among the independent republics of the Union was thus preserved. ROSTA, by name, vanished from the international scene into the obscurity of just another national agency.

Essentially this was a paper reorganization. To the subscribers and news agency executives abroad, there was no apparent difference. The ROSTA correspondents remained in their posts, and the exchange agreements with foreign news agencies were not amended to indicate a change in name or status. The director of ROSTA just put on a second hat as head of the Telegrafnoe Agentstvo Sovetskogo Soiuza, or TASS.

The agreements between ROSTA and Reuters and Havas had fallen by the wayside in the early post-revolution period although, as indicated above, there was some cooperation. ROSTA, as early as 1922, entered into an exchange agreement with the United Press, an independent American agency that had crashed the Latin American market during the war when the Associated Press refused to violate the cartel agreement giving Latin American rights to Havas. But the Soviet Union was interested in international respectability and jettisoned its agreement with UP when it appeared that one way to negotiate with Great Britain for recognition was through freezing out the upstart United Press, which was harassing Reuters throughout the world. It was not until 1933 that the head of TASS concluded agreements with the Associated Press and United Press and would no longer deal with the cartel as a group.

TASS, to all intents and purposes, emerged from the national agency stage to that of a full-fledged international news agency on an equal footing with the Associated Press, United Press, Reuters, and Havas in the early 1930s. It had exchange agreements not only with the big four but with the score of national agencies that had sprung up in Europe.

The origins of today's socialist agencies are not to be found in TASS, however, but in the crumbling Austro-Hungarian Empire and the ashes of Wolff. Historically, the Austro-Hungarian Empire had regarded news agencies and newspapers as instruments of national policy. The first national news agency in Middle Europe, the K. K. Telegraphen Korrespondenz Bureau, was founded by the Ministry of Commerce of the old empire and had exclusive news distribution rights for Austria and Hungary under the international news cartel. When one considers that the dual monarchy also issued all the newspapers within its borders, it is apparent that the media of communication were firmly anchored to the state.

When the dual monarchy was carved up into separate countries after World War I, the new governments created their own national agencies almost as soon as the ink on their constitutions dried.

The Bulgarski Telegrafitscheka Agentzia was started in 1918, as an information service with close ties to Havas. Similarly, the Ceska Tiskova Kancelar (CTK or Ceteka) was started in 1918 to provide news of the new democracy and serve as a unifying force for the multilanguage press within its awkward borders. Poland followed suit. Hungary had been served by the Magyar Tavirati Iroda (MTI) since 1881, when it was a private agency competing with KKTK; MTI found itself the national agency of new Hungary, a conglomerate formed by the dissolution of KKTK in Budapest and the confiscation of its assets by the new government. MTI, as a government agency, did not survive the fall of the first Hungarian regime. The Horthy government turned the agency over to private hands, and it became a joint-stock company in 1921.

Romania's national agency was begun under private ownership in 1919. Rador, created in that year by a Bucharest banker, was bought by the Romanian Ministry of Foreign Information in 1924. It was reorganized the following year as a semigovernmental corporation with the state owning 60 percent of the shares. It acted as a publicity channel for the Romanian monarchy in its wheeling and dealing, especially in the era marked by Queen Marie's public relations ventures in search of international financial support. If TASS were to be considered the propaganda vehicle of socialism during this decade, then Rador's role was that of a propagandist for the feudal capitalism of Romania. Most of Rador's correspondents abroad were press attaches in the Romanian embassies and legations. Rador had exchange agreements with Havas and Reuters, and later with Hitler's DNB (Deutsches Nachrichtenburo) and Mussolini's Agenzia Telegrafica Stefani.

The year 1919 also saw the creation of the Avalla agency as the information channel of the press section of the Yugoslav Ministry of Foreign Affairs. Its messages were aimed primarily at the diplomatic corps and the government departments. It issued a daily news bulletin and circulated official notices. It was reorganized in 1924 as a state agency and distributed a national news service in Serbo-Croatian and Slovene to the Yugoslav press. A further reorganization in 1929 turned Avalla into a joint-stock company, with 90 percent of the shares owned by the state and 10 percent by the Yugoslav newspapers. The agency was subsidized by the government in return for mandatory distribution of all official statements. [20]

Avalla expanded internationally in the decade between the wars, signing exchange agreements with Havas, Reuters, Wolff, Stefani, and TASS. It also opened bureaus in Paris, London, Vienna, Warsaw, and Rome. The offices abroad appeared to reflect specific national interests. For example, it closed its offices in Berlin, Vienna, Warsaw, and Rome in 1929 and opened bureaus in Sofia, Athens, Ankara, Bucharest, and Tirana.

In Germany the situation was slightly different. Wolff had been weakened tremendously as an international agency, retaining its correspondents in German cities and in Paris, Rome, London, New York, and Buenos Aires. It did manage to retrieve some Balkan clients such as Yugoslavia and Romania, but its supremacy in Germany was being challenged by an agency founded in 1921 by the Hugenberg Trust. Hugenberg, a giant in German publishing, owned newspapers and magazines as well as several small agencies that were consolidated under the name of the Telegraphen Union (TU). It served the newspapers of

the trust and signed exchange agreements with the Associated Press,
United Press, and the British Exchange Telegraph.

In 1933 the Hitler regime ordered the merger of all German news
agencies to form the Deutsches Nachrichtenburo (DNB). DNB was truly
an instrument of national policy. In addition to its monopoly of the distribution of news in the Third Reich, it instituted an overseas service
in English, French, and German and concluded exchange agreements
with Havas and Reuters.

The zones of news influence changed rapidly between 1929 and 1938.
Reuters had perfected a multiaddress radio system whereby messages
could be transmitted simultaneously at a lower rate. It meant that
Middle European and Balkan agencies could now receive the Reuters
service direct from the source. Czechoslovakia and Romania appeared
to prefer the Havas transmissions, while the other agencies showed increasing interest in Reuters. TASS was a poor third in wooing clients. [21]

Regardless of their previous affiliations, World War II found all the
agencies of Eastern Europe in the camp of DNB—a move that started at
the time Hitler marched into Austria and replaced that country's national
agency with DNB. As tools of Germany's allies, the Hungarian MTI,
the Romanian Rador, and the Bulgarian Telegraph Agency cooperated
completely with DNB and relied upon it exclusively for world news.

As soon as Czechoslovakia and Yugoslavia were occupied by German forces, the DNB service became the sole link between Ceteka and
Avalla and the outside world. The military governments in these nations
did not treat the national agencies with the consideration given to Ritzaus or the Norsk Telegrambyra. (The occupying forces in Denmark and
Norway permitted the national agencies to function throughout the war.
The agencies, however, agreed to the Nazi stipulation that DNB would
be the sole source of foreign news.) The agencies were taken over completely, turning them into translation centers for the DNB reports, and
transmitting messages under the national agencies' logotypes.

Albania, the only country not under German control, came under the
domination of the Italian forces. It had no national news agency, but
Stefani, the Mussolini regime's agency, instituted a special service for
the practically nonexistent Albanian press. [22]

To combat the propaganda efforts of the Nazis and the Fascists, the
resistance movements in Albania, Slovakia, and Yugoslavia created
their own agencies and operated them in a manner similar to the Polish
PAP (Polska Agencja Prasowa), which had been created to serve the
clandestine press and to broadcast news to the outside world.

The news agencies of the resistance forces provided TASS with its
first real chance to crack the Reuters-Havas hold on Eastern Europe,
and it took full advantage of that opportunity. The TASS voice broadcasts from Moscow at dictation speed found ready listeners among the
socialists operating mimeograph machines and hand presses behind the
enemy lines. As the Soviet troops rolled into Mitteleuropa it was obvious
that a new alignment of political zones of influence was in the making
and that it would be matched by the national news agencies.

THE SOCIALIST NEWS AGENCIES OF POSTWAR EUROPE

TASS emerged from World War II relatively unscathed—in fact, its physical facilities had been improved through the acquisition of German telecommunications equipment. TASS also moved rapidly into the minor vacuum in Eastern Europe caused by the disappearance of Havas (a victim of collaboration with the Germans).

The Deutsches Nachrichtenburo and Stefani were eliminated and their facilities acquired by the Allied military governments. Germany, divided into four zones, found itself with four "national" news agencies reflecting the character and news policies of the occupying forces. The Americans established DANA, the Deutsche Nachrichten Agentur, at Bad Nauheim in 1945 and it immediately concluded exchange agreements with the Associated Press and United Press. The British-sponsored Deutscher Pressedienst (DPD) was set up in Hamburg in the same year, distributing Reuters news, while the French supported the Rheina Agency at Baden Baden. It was one of the first foreign clients of Agence France-Presse, which had taken over the facilities of Havas. The Russians fared best, falling heir to what was left of the DNB installation in East Berlin, and established Sowjetische Nachrichtenburo, which distributed TASS dispatches.

It was not until 1949 that the Allied powers permitted the German press of their zones to establish a single West German national agency, Deutsche Presse Agentur (DPA), at Hamburg. Inasmuch as the Western allies had licensed individuals to publish newspapers, there was no problem in establishing a cooperatively owned agency. In East Germany, where newspaper licenses had been granted to political parties and organizations, the creation of Allgemeiner Deutscher Nachrichtendienst (ADN) was the result of joint action by the newspaper units of the Socialist Union Party, Christian Democratic Union, Liberal Democratic Party, National Democratic Party, Democratic Peasant Federation, and Trade Unions Federation, among others.

During the four-year period in which the German news agencies achieved their political, economic, and media foundations, the socialist agencies in other countries were regrouping and establishing the patterns they were to adopt in the years to come. A brief recapitulation of the status of the news agencies in the socialist countries (1945-49) of Europe follows. [23]

Country-by-Country Survey

Albania

As previously indicated, no national news agency worthy of the name existed in Albania prior to World War II. The Albanian Telegraph

Agency (ATA) was established in 1945. It is a state agency with a monopoly of news distribution in Albania. TASS originally was the major source of foreign news for ATA, but with the schism ATA turned to the New China News Agency for a large share of its political news budget. ATA retained its exchange agreements with the news agencies of other socialist countries.

Bulgaria

The Bulgarski Telegrafitscheka Agentzia (BTA), founded as a semi-official news agency in 1918, was officially proclaimed the national news agency of the republic in 1945. At the war's end, the chief international source of news for the Bulgarian News Agency was Reuters.

Czechoslovakia

Ceska Tiskova Kancelar (Ceteka), founded in 1918, was taken over by the Germans during World War II and used as a transmission belt for DNB dispatches. Its revival as a democratic agency was preceded by Zpravodajska Agentima Slovenska (ZAS), founded shortly after the establishment of the independent state of Slovakia in 1943. ZAS was an organ of the Commissariat of Slovakian Information and was financed by it. The agency occupied the premises and utilized the equipment originally installed by Ceteka and taken over by the Germans. After the liberation of Prague, ZAS worked closely with Ceteka and essentially operated as a local branch of it. The Czech news agency transmitted Slovak news abroad and delivered world news to ZAS for distribution to the Slovak press and radio station. Ceteka had agreements with Reuters, AFP, AP, and TASS.

Hungary

Magyar Tavirati Iroda (MTI), which became a joint-stock company in 1921, developed into a communication giant prior to World War II, embracing not only the telegraph news agency but also the Hungarian Broadcasting Company, the Hungarian Film Bureau, and the Hungarian Advertising Agency. It was taken over by the Central Hungarian Information Office in 1945. It emerged as a government agency rather than an organ of the state inasmuch as the majority of its shares were owned by the political parties that formed the coalition government. It signed agreements with TASS, Reuters, AFP, and AP for the exchange of news.

Poland

Polska Agencja Prasowa (PAP) had its origins in the Soviet campaign to reoccupy Polish territories. PAP was founded in 1943 by the Union of Polish Patriots, the Russian answer to London's Polish government-in-exile. PAP advanced with the Soviet troops. The first stop was Lublin, then the liberated right bank of Warsaw, next a retreat to Lodz, and finally the return to the capital in time to frustrate the efforts in London to reestablish the old agency. In 1945 PAP was confirmed as a state-owned and operated enterprise and entered into exchange agreements with Reuters, AFP, and TASS.

Romania

Rador, which had been a semiofficial agency of the Romanian monarchy, served as a German transmission belt during World War II and resumed activities as a private agency in 1945. According to a Romanian editor who worked for Rador following the war, the agency was subsidized by foreign sources (primarily French) to compete with the struggling Romanian socialist agency. The U. N. study of news agencies makes no mention of this competition but merely states that in "May 1949 Rador was dissolved and its equipment taken over by the new Romanian agency, Agentie de Informatii Telegrafice. "[24]

Agerpres is responsible to the Council of Ministers; its directors and deputy directors are appointed by the council. The agency has exchange agreements with AFP, AP, Reuters, and TASS.

Yugoslavia

The Telegrafska Agencija Nova Jugoslavija (Tanjug) reflects its political environment. It was organized in 1943 on the foundation laid by the resistance news services. It differs from the Soviet model in that it is not attached to the Council of Ministers but is a cooperative organization headed by a director and executive board nominated by the chairman of the Council for Science and Culture. Tanjug had exchange agreements with AFP, Reuter, UPI, and TASS.

Current Influence of TASS

Despite the favorable climate for TASS created by its World War II transmissions to the resistance agencies, the national news agencies of the coalition governments did not favor TASS. An analysis of the sources of news in the press of three socialist countries by Vladimir Dedijer, a Yugoslav journalist and member of the U. N. Commission on Freedom of Information, verifies this initial opposition to TASS reports even on the part of the Communist Party press. Dedijer checked Rude Pravo, the central organ of the Communist Party of Czechoslovakia, and found that from mid-1947 to mid-1948 some 80 percent of its news on foreign affairs came from national sources and only 3 percent from TASS. Four years later, the proportion of such news coming from non-TASS

sources fell to under 44 percent, while TASS news rose to 46 percent.
In Romania, the growth of TASS-originated news rose from 30 percent in
1947 to 75 percent in 1952. In Bulgaria it went up from 20.6 percent to
64.5 percent. [25]

One explanation of Dedijer's findings may be that the political atmosphere was such that the editors were relatively free to pursue their
own sources of news, and that the rise of Titoism and the Stalinist reaction affected the news-gathering picture. Another explanation is found
in frequent one-line references in the UNESCO study: "In October 1950,
it [referring to the Bulgarian socialist agency] signed an agreement by
which its activities were co-ordinated with those of TASS . . . . Since
that date, TASS Hellcasts* are almost the sole source from which the
Bulgarian agency obtains its foreign news. "[26] Similar observations are
made for other socialist agencies.

The UNESCO study does not state the place of this conference of
socialist news agencies at which all the agencies signed similar agreements. The deputy director of Agerpres denied that such a meeting had
taken place when asked about it by this author in spring 1958. A search
of the U.S. Library of Congress and inquiries to UNESCO during the
preparation of this essay uncovered no documentation. The only evidence was of general information and turned up in the New York Times
of September 2, 1950:

> PRAGUE, Czechoslovakia, Sept. 1 (AP)--Vaclav Korinek,
> new general manager of the official Czech News Agency (CTK),
> said today that it would follow the pattern set by TASS, the
> official Soviet news agency. Mr Korinek succeeds Milos
> Novotny, who has reached the age of 63.

Current Structure

Today, the news agencies of the socialist countries are structured
differently from those of the 1950s. The rise of China and the spread
of Hsin Hua's influence not only in Asia but throughout the rest of the
world is one factor. The New China News Agency is well on its way to
becoming an international news agency. The signing of news agreements
with Associated Press and United Press International following the Nixon
visit to China completed Hsin Hua's complement of international agency
ties, which previously were confined to AFP, Reuters, and TASS. It has
also added to the number of bureaus abroad, including New York and
Geneva. Most news agencies of the socialist countries have exchange
agreements with it.

---

*A form of transmission utilizing the German-made Hellschreiber
apparatus.

Another factor is the increased use of dispatches furnished by the international agencies such as AFP, Reuters, AP, and UPI. Most of the socialist agencies have had agreements with two or more of the international agencies, but in the past the information was used mostly for background purposes.

A third factor may be the increased use of material available through exchange agreements with other socialist news agencies as well as the national news agencies of the capitalist countries.

But most important, in this writer's judgment, is the fact that the news agency structure itself has changed and national agencies have become viable in the news-gathering sense.

ADN, the news agency of the German Democratic Republic, is typical of this self-sufficiency. It could cover the world, with several exceptions, through its own correspondents if it chose to do so. It is apparent that it elects to do so in the major capitals. ADN does not rely upon exchange agreements to cover Bonn; it has its own correspondent permanently stationed there. East Germany obtains its United Nations news directly from the ADN correspondent in New York. Similarly, ADN has its own correspondents at Geneva, European headquarters of the United Nations system and scores of other international organizations, and at Brussels, headquarters of the European Common Market.

A regional tally of ADN correspondents throughout the world would show coverage in London, Paris, Stockholm, Copenhagen, Vienna, Rome, and Amsterdam for Western Europe; Budapest, Bucharest, Belgrade, Moscow, Prague, Sofia, and Warsaw for Eastern Europe; Algiers, Conakry, and Dar-es-Salaam for Africa; Beirut, Cairo, Baghdad, Damascus, and Khartoum for the Arab area; Djakarta, New Delhi, Hanoi, Peking, and Rangoon for Asia; and Havana, Lima, Mexico City, Montevideo, and Santiago de Chile for Latin America.

Does ADN make use of the dispatches sent by its correspondents? Interviews with the head of the agency's English desk in East Berlin and with the ADN correspondent in New York indicated that ADN regards its correspondents the same way American agencies do. The agency prefers using its own material and will feature its correspondents' stories. ADN's coverage is typical and the same pattern is to be found in the other socialist agencies, depending upon the individual agency requirements.

It is apparent from the foregoing inventory of news sources that the national agencies of the socialist countries are not bound to one fountainhead for their news flow. The editors of the national news agencies can select from the raw material the story that will be transmitted to the nation's news media. In this sense the editors of all national news agencies throughout the world are brothers under the skin, for they are the gatekeepers and decide what goes out.

The gatekeeper role of the news agency and newspaper editor has been the subject of numerous studies in the United States. The news agency editor has a number of options. He has at his command three or four reports from different agencies including that of his own correspondent. Option one is obvious: The editor will feature the report of his own correspondent and add sidebars from the other stories. Option two may be AP, Reuter, TASS, or AFP versions of the same story. The experienced editor knows which agency will have a better story at that particular moment; it may be that he is familiar with the ability of one agency's correspondent and prefers to ride with him, or it may be that another agency is better in treating economic stories. A third option is to consider the politics of the nation involved. The American agency editor will seldom use a TASS story from Moscow without referring to a Western agency's report, and vice versa. This may pose a problem for the editor of a socialist agency if his own correspondent has not reported the story.

The editor of a daily newspaper in the socialist countries examined in this study has available to him, with rare exceptions, the service of one agency: the national agency. The role of the socialist newspaper editor, as a gatekeeper, is thus a limited one. He, of course, has the option to use (or not use) the national agency's report. The international news has been digested and this is the only version he receives—unless his paper happens to be one of the very few with its own foreign correspondents.

Contrast this with the material available to the foreign editor of a prestige newspaper such as the New York Times. He has at his disposal not only the reports of Times correspondents stationed in most major capitals but also the reports of AP, UPI, Reuters, AFP, and TASS. It is a plethora of news riches on most occasions, but the Times feels justified in spending large sums of money to make certain it has access to all the news, all the time.

If there is a conclusion to be drawn, it is an obvious one, that the foreign editor of the New York Times has a far greater role as gatekeeper than his colleague on Neues Deutschland. It is equally obvious from the evidence cited in this essay that the foreign editor of a socialist news agency and the foreign editor of a Western news agency are brothers under the skin. They have equal access to international news sources (in most instances to the same sources); what they do with the material is something else.

It is difficult to obtain precise data concerning the gatekeeper role in the socialist news agencies. This author has found little in the way of literature concerning this aspect of international communication.

While preparing this essay the author came across one aspect of the gatekeeper role, in connection with the press reports of Marshal Zhukov's death. The Paris-based International Herald Tribune printed an Associated Press dispatch datelined Moscow, June 18, as follows:

> Rumors circulated here today that retired Soviet Marshal
> Georgi Zhukov, Russia's most decorated soldier, had died.
> The news agency Tass, however, denied the reports.

According to the reports, Marshal Zhukov, 77, died after
an illness. He suffered a severe heart attack a few years ago
and [has] since been living in retirement at his country home
outside Moscow.

Queried about the rumors, Moscow radio spokesmen said
the reports were not true and added that they had received no
such information.

A Western report said Marshal Zhukov's death would be
announced by Moscow television this evening. But there was
no such announcement.

A ranking official of the Defense Ministry newspaper,
Krasnaya Zvezda (Red Star), said it had no plans to publish
an obituary tomorrow morning.

Earlier today, an unofficial source reported that Marshal
Zhukov died in the Kremlin hospital after suffering a heart
attack. The source said he had been hospitalized there
since December and had recently suffered four other heart
attacks.

Evidently the press agencies of the socialist countries ignored the
Associated Press report—at least in the ADN and Ceteka transmissions.
ADN's report of the death of Marshal Zhukov appeared in the June 20
issues of Neues Deutschland and the Berliner Zeitung, carrying a Moscow dateline of June 19. The Ceteka report, datelined Moscow, June 19,
appeared in Rude Pravo on June 20.

The reports transmitted by ADN and Ceteka were filed by their own
correspondents in Moscow.

The New York Times, like ADN and Ceteka, did not have a report
from its own Moscow correspondent until June 19, but he did stress what
he had learned unofficially as follows:

The marshal died after a heart attack in the Kremlin Hospital
but his death was not officially announced until today (June
19). He reportedly had been hospitalized since December and
had suffered several heart attacks, unofficial sources said.

The New York Times, however, with its direct access to Associated
Press—which Neues Deutschland could have had only if ADN had wished
to distribute it—was able to carry the AP report in its issue of June 19.
The Times, of course, used the complete text of its correspondent's
report as soon as it became available.

The incident cited above may appear to disprove the writer's con-
tention that there has been a convergence in the news agencies of the
socialist and capitalist countries. This does not necessarily follow.
What is apparent is that the socialist and capitalist news agencies have
equal access to international news but they still are bound by their respective concepts of news. The capitalist news agencies are more apt

to risk the possibility of a report turning sour in the interest of speed, information, and competition, while the socialist news agencies (and some Western national agencies) are reluctant to rely upon nonofficial news sources.

NOTES

1. Graham Storey, Reuters' Century, 1851-1951 (London: Parrish, 1951), p. 46.

2. UNESCO, News Agencies (Paris, 1953), pp. 160-61.

3. Storey, Reuters, p. 50.

4. Svend Thorsen, Newspapers in Denmark (Copenhagen: Danske selskab, 1953), p. 47.

5. Ibid. , p. 48.

6. Storey, Reuters, p. 51.

7. Ibid. , p. 52.

8. UNESCO, News Agencies, p. 18.

9. N. G. Pal'gunov, Osnovy informatzii v gazete: TASS i ego rol' (Moscow: Izdatel'stvo Moskovskogo universiteta, 1955), p. 18.

10. Ibid., , p. 25.

11. Ibid. , p. 26.

12. Storey, Reuters, p. 165.

13. Boris Chekhonin, "TASS—Tverskii Boulevard 10, " The Democratic Journalist, April 1974, pp. 3-4.

14. Interview with Nicholas Kirilov, April 1958, Paris.

15. Theodore E. Kruglak, The Two Faces of TASS (2nd ed.; Westport, Conn.: Greenwood Press, 1972), p. 18.

16. Pal'gunov, TASS, pp. 27-28.

17. Kruglak, TASS, p. 19.

18. Frederick L. Schuman, Soviet Politics, at Home and Abroad (New York: Alfred A. Knopf, 1946), p. 293.

19. Schuman, Soviet Politics, pp. 295-96.

20. UNESCO, News Agencies, pp. 103-9, 141-44.

21. Kruglak, TASS, p. 52.

22. Carlo Ventura, La Stampa a Trieste, 1943-45 (Udine, Italy: Del Bianco, 1958), p. 9.

23. The material in this section was obtained by the writer through interviews in East Berlin, Warsaw, and Bucharest, in 1972-73, and from UNESCO, News Agencies.

24. UNESCO, News Agencies, p. 143.

25. International Press Institute, The Press in Authoritarian Countries (Zurich, 1959), p. 74.

26. UNESCO, News Agencies, p. 103.

INFORMATION POLICY AND
OPERATION OF THE
TANJUG NEWS AGENCY
Michel Kwiatkowski

The aim of this essay is to present and to analyze the operations and the information policy of the Yugoslav news agency Tanjug. The information policy of Tanjug and that of the government are not the same, but similar, because of a sort of personal union of the agency staff and top executives of the Party and state establishment. This essay analyzes the principal geopolitical tendencies of the agency and the methods it uses to promote the basic lines of Yugoslav policy: solidarity of the nonaligned countries abroad; originality of the self-management, one-party system; and the spirit of togetherness in the Yugoslav federation.

There are several reasons to choose the Yugoslav agency as the object of research. First, Yugoslavia offers a unique example of a nonaligned socialist state, neither great power nor Soviet ally, which justifies our belief that news produced by its national agency is not necessarily conditioned by a situation of bloc (Warsaw Pact) or of axis (Tirana-Peking) and that it may generally be influenced by solely Yugoslav factors. This means that neither Soviet nor Chinese pressure is exercised on the staff of the agency. In this respect even self-censorship is nonexistent. Second, Yugoslav press legislation is more highly developed than that of the other Eastern countries, and it is also the most liberal. [1] The news agency is included in the self-management system that prevails in Yugoslav enterprises; as a result, it enjoys a certain amount of administrative and economic independence from the state. For these reasons, Tanjug offers ideal conditions to study the influence of the pressure—always discernible but often hard to define—that any one-party political system puts on the news. It may seem rather naive to talk about "influenced news," which implies the existence of "pure news." There is obviously no such thing as pure news, for news is always made up of arbitrarily chosen facts. When we use this term we are referring to the truthfulness with which facts are presented, and not to the choice of facts. Finally, the agency's output is impressive because of its originality. Unlike the other "little" Eastern news agencies, Tanjug's dispatches are not limited to news directly concerning its country of origin. Nor do they contain, like those of TASS and Hsin Hua, a mixture of news about world events and propaganda.

In fact, the dispatches that the Yugoslav agency sends abroad are deserving of the closest attention. In this field, specifically, the agency seems to demonstrate most clearly its originality. Generally speaking, its domestic service carries translations of dispatches from the large worldwide agencies, and if Tanjug serves as a transmission belt for official circles, it seldom acts as a censor. Moreover, it does not have a monopoly of international news comparable to that of PAP or Ceteka. The Yugoslav press sends a considerable number of correspondents abroad, and the foreign press—especially the Western press—is freely available in Yugoslavia.

HISTORICAL BACKGROUND

Throughout its history, the development of the national news agency has reflected the evolution of Yugoslav society itself, from the time of the struggle against the German occupation, through the orthodox Communist period and the onset of the self-management system, to the appearance of the new federal regime in the 1970s.

Telegrafska Agencija Nova Jugoslavija (Tanjug) was created on October 4, 1943, in Jajce, Bosnia, as a military news service attached to the headquarters of the Liberation Army of Yugoslavia. [2] It was founded by Mosa Pijade, a communist intellectual and journalist, to publicize as widely as possible the second session of the anti-fascist Council for the National Liberation of Yugoslavia (AVNOJ) and Tito's federalist program. A team of fifteen led by Slobodan Ribnikar, an eminent journalist before the war, put out a daily bulletin of 400 copies destined for Yugoslav liberation forces and their allies, and the team also monitored foreign radio broadcasts. This core of the agency followed the army headquarters from place to place, and in the process five journalists lost their lives during a German parachutist attack at Drvar in January 1944. In the fall of the same year the staff moved to Belgrade, where it took over part of the prewar agency Avalla.

After the liberation, the whole Yugoslav press operation was reorganized after the image of the Soviet press. Until December 1945 prewar newspapers were purely and simply confiscated. The new publications, financed by the state, were filled with the leaders' speeches, with anti-Western propaganda and with calls for the country's reconstruction. In 1945 a law proclaimed freedom of the press and free access to foreign newspapers, but in practice it was not applied. [3]

In the same way, Tanjug was modeled after the Soviet news agency TASS. It became a state institution, financed by the federal budget, and its production was destined above all for goverment agencies, while the press remained a secondary client. During this period the agency ful-filled three functions: distributing news abroad, gathering news from abroad, and diffusing propaganda favorable to the regime. Its news was as tendentious as that of the other Eastern agencies, [4] and for the same reason: All these news agencies worked according to the directives of the agitation and propaganda department of the Party's Central Committee.

For the press, the revision of the Marxist-Leninist-Stalinist dogma in the 1950s and the rejection of the Soviet model resulted in relative economic independence accompanied by a cut in state aid, which in turn led to a drop of 40 percent in publication figures. In 1956 press enterprises began to be managed by workers' councils, elected by the workers themselves but also equipped with a publishing council designed to represent "society's interests," which in fact serves to assure the state's political control.

The news agency Tanjug, however, lagged behind this evolution toward self-management. Although it was declared a "financially auton-omous institution" in 1952, it was directed by a "directing committee" composed of 15 members (of which 7 were elected by the workers while 7 others and the director were chosen by the government). The govern-ment was also charged with "supervising the accomplishment of Tanjug's tasks." [5]

Economic autonomy had no immediate effect upon news production since the agency mostly sent out complete texts of official declarations without being allowed to comment on them. However, it began to seek out newspapers willing to subscribe to its services in order to supple-ment government aid. In addition, in the new climate of decentralization and liberalization, competitors began to appear: a cooperative news agency, Jugopress; a photographic agency; and a Chamber of Commerce economic news service. Jugopress sent out one daily and several weekly news bulletins until 1957 when, following a conflict with the authorities, the agency changed its orientation and thereafter limited its activities to interpretive commentary, no longer diffusing news as such. [6] The other two agencies were absorbed by Tanjug in 1960.

During the blockade that the socialist countries imposed in the 1950s, the agency expanded into new regions, reaching China (1952), Egypt (1953), and Sweden (1959). At this time the agency employed about 800 people, of whom more than 100 were journalists. Nevertheless, 80 percent of its news originated from the large news agencies whose ser-vices it received in Belgrade.

At the end of the 1950s, reacting to pressure from its customers—the press, worried about profits, demanded news that would appeal to a wider public—Tanjug obtained the right to process and summarize of-ficial documents. In 1960 an evening edition was instituted to serve evening newspapers and radio stations; it treats wide-ranging and light news such as sports and accidents.

In addition, the reconciliation with the USSR allowed the Yugoslav agency's correspondents to return to the socialist countries from which

they had been expelled between 1949 and 1955. So Tanjug went back to
this area, very important for the Yugoslavs from the geopolitical point
of view. The Yugoslav agency's news from socialist countries will be
described below.

In 1962 a government ordinance defined the agency as an "independent institution" and created a new directing body, the Tanjug council.
At the same time the directing committee was reorganized and the director's role redefined. [7]

The new council was composed of fifteen members. Only three were
chosen directly by the government from among public workers, three
were delegated by the Council for News and Publishing (the press), and
three by the Association of Radio Stations, while five were elected by
the working collective. The director, a member of the council, is always chosen by the government, but he cannot serve either as president
of the council or as president of the directing committee. Therefore, the
agency's customers, with a total of six representatives, have become
the deciding force in the council, or principal managing body; whereas
the directing committee (elected by the workers from among their number,
and the director) is charged only with administering the agency's everyday activities.

This transformation, leading to a certain independence for the agency, resulted secondarily in an unfavorable influence on the enterprise's
precarious financial equilibrium: A tax reduction of 15 percent from
which it had previously benefited was withdrawn. Despite liberal
government measures to grant the agency a tax exemption "as an unusual
measure" for the 1962 fiscal year, its difficulties continued. The staff
was reduced from 800 to 500, while a bonus system was introduced to
stimulate productivity.

All this did not stop Tanjug's international expansion. In 1964 it
launched a vast program of news exchanges among nonaligned countries,
originally involving five African and eleven Asian countries. In the
following years Tanjug correspondents were sent successively to Nai-
robi, Accra, Conakry, and even Melbourne, Australia, the last continent
to be covered by the Yugoslav agency.

Within the agency, the evolution of the balance of forces toward
greater autonomy reached its highest development in 1966. The representation of Tanjug's working collective in the council rose to 25
people, [8] whereas that of the government and the customers remained
unchanged. Moreover, the agency's workers alone decided budgetary
matters. However, this independence was not without its limits. In
1969 a serious conflict arose between Tanjug and the League of Communists of Yugoslavia over the agency's commentary on the LCY's re-
fusal to participate in the world communist conference in Moscow. The
Party described the news as "incomplete and one-sided" and accused
the agency of having spoken in its own name without proper authorization. Tanjug's editor-in-chief, Mojmir Pudar, replied by pleading the
agency's independence, but he nevertheless offered his resignation. [9]

At the beginning of the 1970s Yugoslavia's ever-present centrifugal tendencies intensified. The leaders responded on the one hand by a considerable hardening of policy, and on the other hand by introducing 23 constitutional amendments (June 1971), and three years later, a new constitution allowing a far-reaching decentralization of federal powers. [10] After a certain lag, both phenomena made their impact felt within the agency. As early as the beginning of 1971 the Federal Committee of the Union of Yugoslav Journalists drew up a document stipulating autonomy for offices in the various federated republics and autonomous regions. [11] This proposal must have encountered definite resistance because it was not applied until the summer of 1974. Simultaneously, the government decided to create an "international press center" in Belgrade, within Tanjug, whose task would be to "promote cooperation with mass media organs abroad."[12] This decision may be seen as a desire to compensate for the loss of imporatnce suffered by the Belgrade office as a result of the decentralization of Tanjug's structures.

For Tanjug, the general hardening of political life in Yugoslavia led in July 1974 to yet another change in the council's structure, this time in the direction of greater government control of the agency. Thus the council, which numbers 27 members, is presided over by Lazar Mojsov, a member of the Central Committee of the LCY and vice-minister for foreign affairs. Tanjug's employees are reduced to 7 members. Among the other members are a vice-president of the federal assembly, a member of the executive committee of the presidium of the Socialist Alliance of the Working People of Yugoslavia (the mass organization of the LCY), as well as delegates from all the republics and regions, and from relevant federal bodies. This personal union of the agency and the establishment is also true of the journalists: For instance Jak Koprivc, secretary of information of the republic of Slovenia, was appointed editor-in-chief of Tanjug on September 19, 1974. His predecessor, Teodor Olic, was a member of the Commission for International Relations at the Central Committee of the LCY.

To conclude this description of the Yugoslav news agency's evolution, we may observe that it was characterized by a movement toward independence from the political authorities that hit a ceiling in 1969 before retreating slightly during the 1970s, when an increased number of official representatives were introduced into the directing body but at the same time the decentralization movement continued to make unquestionable progress. From a military body, then a state one, centralized and totally financed by the state, the agency has become formally independent, decentralized, and less financially dependent (although the investments necessary to improve the basic technical equipment are still covered by the state). [13] State bodies also represent half of Tanjug's customers. [14]

We are inevitably led to ask what functions the Yugoslav news agency currently fulfills, both within Yugoslavia and on the international news market.

OPERATIONS

Tanjug currently employs about 500 people, of whom a quarter are journalists. The agency is divided into five sections: foreign desk, domestic desk, photographic service, economic service, and an administrative department that includes research and editing of bulletins. [15]

Every day, Tanjug receives and rewrites 500,000 words of news. It receives foreign news from the 40 news agencies with which it works (including AP, Reuters, and AFP), [16] and from its 37 foreign correspondents seconded by a dozen correspondents it recruits on the spot. Within Yugoslavia it receives news from its head office in Belgrade, from offices in the capitals of the republics, from permanent correspondents in other cities, and from 51 correspondents working under contract. About a third of its news from abroad comes from correspondents whose copy has priority over dispatches received from other news agencies and rewritten at the head office. Within Yugoslavia, the agency sends out a general service and an economic service by teletype. It mails out a bulletin, Red Tanjug, summarizing dispatches from foreign agencies, as well as several economic and specialized bulletins—on the army, youth, international workers' movements, science, culture—and a digest of articles from the most important newspapers all over the world. The photographic service covers only Yugoslavia; it is linked with 25 daily newspapers by a phototelegraphy network.

Tanjug sends six-hour broadcasts abroad twice a day in English and French as well as numerous special broadcasts destined for third world countries such as Mexico and Indonesia. In addition, the agency sends out a bulletin entitled Features in five languages, with a circulation of 1,000.

Tanjug's customers in Yugoslavia are the press (25 daily newspapers, about 50 periodicals, 8 radio and 6 television stations), business firms, of which 1,000 receive the economic service, and some 800 state bodies, including Yugoslav embassies, which receive a special diplomatic service.

To make this data seem less abstract, we may add that the Yugoslav agency ranks in eighth place in the world for the volume of its news (250,000 words daily), coming after the big five (AP, AFP, UPI, Reuters, and TASS), Hsin Hua, and the Egyptian Middle East News Agency (MENA). Now let us turn to an examination of the news sent out from Belgrade.

AGENCY INFORMATION POLICY

I have already alluded to the reasons that led me to focus on news sent abroad. The first is that in my work I am in daily contact with this service, the second lies in the fact that the foreign service better re-

flects Tanjug's characteristic features, since the domestic service is
composed (apart from the foreign service's dispatches) mostly of translations of dispatches from the great worldwide agencies. In order to
define the general orientation of Tanjug's news policy, I have analyzed
all its dispatches during the months of March and July 1974. In addition,
I have compared and analyzed all significant phenomena observed in
Tanjug's news diffused between May 1973 and May 1974.

Geopolitical Tendencies

From the very beginning of the analysis it became evident that, in
order to understand Tanjug's orientations, we must distinguish between
two functions fulfilled by the agency: Specifically, we must distinguish
between foreign news treating Yugoslav diplomats and delegations, and
news concerning only third world countries; in other words, between the
diplomatic function and the news function. In order to study the latter, I
drew up a list of countries mentioned in nondiplomatic dispatches and
divided them into three groups: Western, socialist, and third world
countries.

Dispatches from abroad represent 40 to 50 percent of Tanjug's total
news output. Nondiplomatic dispatches (which, as I have said, do not
bear upon Yugoslav affairs) make up 60 to 75 percent of the news from
abroad. In studying this nondiplomatic news, which alone reflects the
agency's policy as opposed to that of Yugoslav diplomacy, I did not
count the dispatches but the number of times a country was mentioned.
Thus, if a dispatch concerned, for example, Soviet-American relations
commented upon by an Indian newspaper, this news was classified in
categories concerning the United States, the Soviet Union, and India.
The results of this research were examined by dividing the countries
mentioned into three groups: industrial countries (North America,
Western Europe, Australia, Japan, Turkey, Greece, and the Republic of
South Africa); socialist countries (the Soviet Union and its allies, China,
North Korea, and Cuba); and the third world. The respective figures for
these three groups were 97, 82, 112 for March, and 183, 72, 323 for
July 1974. It should be pointed out that in July the Cyprus affair increased the mentions of the third world (Cyprus was cited 122 times)
and of the Western countries (Greece and Turkey were cited 79 times
against 15 in March). However, even taking into account these events,
which disturbed the balance of relations between the three groups, the
predominance of the third world in Tanjug's dispatches is clearly evident, as is a slight superiority of the Western world as compared to the
socialist countries.

This observation was confirmed by the relationship among dispatches concerning various international organizations, which were
studied separately. Again, news about Latin America, Africa, the Arab
countries, decolonization, and above all the movement of nonaligned

countries, in general shows a clear quantitative superiority over news
treating the European Economic Community, NATO, and so on. But organizations of the socialist countries, the Warsaw Treaty, and Comecon
were not mentioned a single time during the two months studied.

Tanjug's foreign service can thus be immediately defined as according priority to news about the third world and, contrary to what we might
expect, as oriented rather more toward the West than toward the socialist
camp. However, it seems necessary to add a few observations about
the quality of the news concerning each group of countries.

Quality of News

The dispatches about capitalist countries generally fall into the
category of hard news, and it would be difficult to discern a difference
between a dispatch from AP or Reuters and one from Tanjug. Unlike TASS
or Hsin Hua, Tanjug does not accord excessive publicity to economic
or other difficulties in the West or to strikes or crime. A frequent subject in these dispatches is that of conditions accorded to immigrant
workers in the West, but the emphasis is usually on the advantages
granted them in one or another of the host countries, as, for example,
in a news item about a Yugoslav worker's membership in a Swedish
committee for immigrant workers. Such news, I think, answers the need
of maintaining the relationship between the Yugoslav state and its people
working abroad and confirms the approval of economic emigration, which
is contrary to the practice of other socialist countries.

Dispatches about communist countries, although less numerous,
are of greater interest to the world information market than the preceding
category. Yugoslav journalists manage to penetrate the closed circles
of the Soviet and Chinese establishment more easily than their Western
colleagues, and they know how to take advantage of this. Thus, Tanjug
was the only news agency to announce ahead of time that the plenum
of the Soviet Central Committee, meeting in July 1974, would not effect
any changes in the Politburo or government, while the Western news
agencies spoke of the possible departure of Suslov and Pel'she. Once
again, Tanjug's correspondent was the only one of 200 foreign observers
in Moscow who mentioned Mikoyan's departure from the Presidium of the
Supreme Soviet, the last official post he held. The same is true of news
about China. Tanjug's editor predicted Chairman Mao's intervention in
the campaign against Lin Piao and Confucius two weeks before it was
announced by the People's Daily. [17] Although it remained neutral to the
point of only once mentioning—and even then with the utmost discretion—
Alexander Solzhenitsyn's expulsion from the Soviet Union, Tanjug is
nevertheless an invaluable means of gaining information about both
communist great powers.

Tanjug's attitude toward the other socialist countries is less cir-
cumspect. A dispatch from Bucharest on March 28, 1974, furnishes an

eloquent example. The lead of this news item, which comments on the resignation of Romanian Premier Georghe Maurer, stated: "Those who leave, it is usually thought, do not reconcile themselves easily to that fact and therefore do it with opposition and under pressure." But, continued the Tanjug correspondent, "Things seem to have been quite the opposite in case of ex-Prime Minister Maurer: he himself asked to quit the office." The Yugoslav journalist, who quotes Maurer as saying that his request stemmed from "a profound confrontation with himself," suggests by this unusual manner of presenting Maurer's dismissal, never encountered in the practice of news agencies either occidental or socialist, that the reality of his dismissal might differ from the premier's statement. Such was the feeling of the AFP journalists.

Bulgaria is the only country that the Yugoslav news agency frequently criticizes for its attitude toward the Yugoslav Republic, especially apropos the Macedonian conflict, which has set Sofia against Belgrade for more than twenty years. It recently denounced a Bulgarian encyclopedia and a film for "presenting in a one-sided way" Macedonian history and the liberation of Yugoslav territory from the Nazi occupation.

It is difficult to evaluate correctly dispatches about the third world. As we mentioned above, this group is the focus of the greatest number of nondiplomatic dispatches, and it determines Tanjug's principal function as one of diffusing news from the developing countries. This news is concentrated around several distinct axes: meetings of nonaligned countries, whose activities and documents receive the greatest publicity; Middle East problems; and relations between developing and industrial countries. Now it may seem normal for the Yugoslav agency to make a point of giving greater coverage to the nonaligned countries' policy statements and to the attitudes of the developing countries than to those of other countries (for example, concerning the conflict brought about by Common Market limitations of beef imports). But the news about the Middle East gives rise to certain reservations about objectivity.

Behavior in Conflict Situations

First of all, dispatches about the conflict between Israel and the Arab countries originate exclusively in the latter, which can hardly contribute to their objectivity. In the second place, although Tanjug receives the services of several large Western news agencies, in certain rare cases it not only ignores their content but goes so far as to denounce their news as "Zionist propaganda." The most flagrant illustration was coverage of the Israeli-Arab war of October 1973. After announcing the onset of hostilities as reported in bulletins from the Egyptian news agency MEN—as a result of which headlines in the Yugoslav afternoon press on October 6, 1973, read "Israel Attacks Egypt and Syria"[18]—Tanjug sent out a dispatch from its Paris correspondent entitled "Propaganda Action," worded as follows:

During the afternoon all Western information media were
flooded by various announcements and communiques, which
came either directly from Israel, or from quarters and centers
in the world close to Israel . . . . The principal task of this
large-scale propaganda action . . . is to present Arab countries as aggressors . . . . But it has not achieved the desired
effect.

It should be added that a dispatch from Beirut sent out two hours
after the first announcements said that it was "impossible to establish
who was first to open fire." However, despite its capital importance,
this sentence appeared only at the top of the dispatch's second page.

This description of Tanjug's news sent to foreign countries must be
completed by a study of the image of Yugoslavia that the news agency
presents. First, it must be stressed that the official declarations and
press reviews that the agency reproduces are not necessarily lacking in
interest, especially if we compare them to analogous documents from
the other socialist countries, for Yugoslav political life is much richer
and more public than that of the other one-party countries. Nevertheless,
a detailed study of certain dispatches leads to the conclusion that the
image of the country as presented by Tanjug is incomplete.

A news item dated October 6, 1973, from Belgrade, announced that
Vojin Lukic, former federal Secretary of the Interior, was condemned to
two and a half years of imprisonment for "the criminal offense of hostile
propaganda." The item, which referred to Lukic's trial, did not specify
the acts he had committed. This omission cannot be attributed to professional inefficiency, for Tanjug's dispatches are of high quality and
usually include analysis and background material.

The presentation of the new law on the foreign press offers an even
more striking example. On July 16, 1974, AFP indicated that this text
forbids foreign correspondents from conducting interviews and public
opinion polls among Yugoslav people or organizations. Tanjug describes the same law as designed to "ensure the representatives of
foreign communications media of special facilities for a wider exchange
of news and communications which will contribute to better mutual
knowledge between Yugoslavia and other countries." Tanjug emphasizes
that "foreign correspondents have the right to communicate with their
news agencies or newspapers without previous authorization" but does
not mention the restrictions announced by AFP.

After this account of the successes and weaknesses of Tanjug, we
come to an examination of the people who produce Yugoslav news, Tanjug's journalists, and also the forces that may influence them.

Journalists

Several generations of journalists cooperate within the Yugoslav
agency. The senior journalists, those who founded Tanjug in 1944, were

both prewar "bourgeois" journalists and resistance members in charge
of news dissemination. After the liberation, the Party's agitation and
propaganda apparatus supplied most of the press administrative staff.
During the 1950s, the Party's hold relaxed and new journalists were
hired and trained within the press enterprises by their more experienced
colleagues. In the absence of professional training centers, the profession began to stagnate and age. This situation changed at the beginning
of the 1960s with the creation of the Journalism Institute of Belgrade and
the Journalism Department at the Political Science Academy of Ljubljana.
Tanjug began to require a university degree and at least one foreign language of its candidates. This policy produced results: 80 percent of the
news agency's journalists possess a degree or at least several years'
university study, whereas this proportion is only 20 percent in the press
in general. [19]

A Tanjug journalist stands to benefit financially if he writes more
and improves his qualifications. His salary is composed of two parts:
a fixed salary represents about 75 percent of his total pay and the re-
mainder comes from piecework renumeration. Introduced at the beginning
of the 1960s, this system is based on points attributed according partly
to the length of the dispatch but mostly to its nature (ordinary dispatch,
synthesis of an event, political analysis, or special feature).

A young journalist entering the agency begins by working on the
national staff. A typical career leads him next to a post as rewrite editor
for news received from abroad. If he wants to be sent abroad as a foreign
correspondent, he has to be selected by his department; the director can
only confirm his nomination. A journalist never spends more than four
years as a foreign correspondent, which on the one hand prevents journalists from stagnation and falling into a rut but also prevents them from
developing specialized knowledge. When he comes back to Belgrade,
the correspondent becomes an editor for news destined to be sent abroad,
which is the highest echelon in Tanjug's hierarchy.

Pressure Groups

The journalists are not limited by institutional censorship in their
work. However, they are subject to a censorship of "advice and instruction" and to the influence of several organizations and forces, of which
the most important is certainly the League of Communists of Yugoslavia,
to which 70 percent of all journalists belong.

The Party, which formerly enjoyed total domination of news presentation through its agit-prop apparatus, nowadays plays the role of
"source of inspiration and adviser" in Yugoslavia. However, it has retained two means of access to Tanjug: (1) The director of the agency,
like all press leaders, is a Party member; (2) 30 percent of the employees, most of them journalists, are Party members; and the Central Committee, and more specifically its Ideological Commission, is an

important customer and purchases news on international workers' movements, which Tanjug has published in a special bulletin since 1964.

Apart from all this, the Party addresses special instructions to its
journalist members. As an example we can quote the "conclusions of the
conference on the militant attitude of Yugoslav news media," organized
by the LCY on November 15, 1973. The document in question, which
Tanjug sent out, calls on all communists working in the news media to
"struggle so that the media will become arms in the service of the working class of Yugoslavia, and in the service of all its peoples and its
nationalities." The LCY exhorts militant journalists to "combat all cases
of laissez-faire, of sitting-on-the-fence attitudes, of editorship without opinion, all things which amount to a sort of resistance to the Party's
policy." Communists must struggle "against technocratic, bureaucratic,
too-liberal ideas, tendencies and practices, and those which go against
the self-management system"; they must combat "their advocates" and
struggle against "attacks launched from abroad against Yugoslavia's
nonaligned foreign policy and against its socialist self-management
orientation." We quote all these propaganda slogans only to point out
the militant nature that the official ideology assigns to the mass media.
The agency, whose task is to relate facts, does not use these terms or,
if it does, puts them in quotation marks.

Another force that may influence a journalist's behavior is his professional organization, the Union of Yugoslav Journalists, which
numbered 4,769 members in 1971, of whom 1,549 worked for daily newspapers, 840 for the radio, 414 for television, 130 for local radio, 369
for news weeklies, 299 for special-interest press, 357 for local news
weeklies, 185 for company house organs, 185 for official news services,
while 66 were freelance journalists, 59 publicists, 37 accredited
foreign correspondents in Belgrade, and 28 film news journalists,
another 120 worked for illustrated reviews, and 221 were retired journalists.[20] The union's existence and activity contributes to the development of a socioprofessional consciousness on the part of the journalists
and to the appearance of ethical standards within the profession. The
latter have been codified in the union's statutes and in a journalism
code.[21] These two documents lay great emphasis on the political commitment of journalism to the Yugoslav form of socialism. Article 8 of the
statutes of the Yugoslav Journalists' Union stipulates that "Any citizen
of the Republic of Yugoslavia may become a member of the Union if he
performs journalistic work favoring general progress and the development
of self-management socialism." The Journalism Code defines the journalist as a "sociopolitical worker" who participates "in the building and
development of socialist society." However, the code elsewhere contains a considerable number of provisions stressing the need for truthful
and objective reporting. Thus, "the journalist, acting according to the
socialist conscience, informs truthfully and faithfully and explains
problems and events in a manysided way." His "social and professional
duty" is to "completely and objectively" inform the workers so that they

can "successfully exercise self-management functions. " In the same way, says the code, the journalist "strives against misleading information and combats all that is untruthful, invented, and unverified. "

Finally, the journalist should also contribute to maintaining a spirit of togetherness in the Yugoslav federation by fighting "bureaucratic, monopolistic, chauvinistic, nationalistic and anti-self-management theses" and militating for "complete respect for the liberty, dignity and equality of all our peoples and nationalities. " In fact, the Yugoslav journalists seem to have managed to strike a balance between political pressure—too general to be really restrictive—and a high degree of professional conscientiousness characterizing a group that has managed to equip itself with a united (because unique) organization, with specific texts stating its commitment to the truth and with bodies charged with seeing that the principles set forth in these texts are respected.

CONCLUSION: OCCASIONAL INFLUENCER

This examination of the agency's production, its organization, and of the journalists' status, allows us to observe that Tanjug's information policy is based on the application of two different methods according to situation. In a quiet time, it supplies the press with current information, in conformity with truth and the journalism code's prinicples. The political pressures stay latent and the influence of the agency is limited to the simple selection of news—in the same sense, we may say, as Associated Press or AFP.

In a time of conflict, in the case of a controversial problem, however, pressure begins to be exerted and the means of influence is tendentious presentation of news, including delaying of information, suppression of some important elements of a news item, or even, exceptionally, introduction of untrue, propaganda elements. The effectiveness of this procedure can be high because of the customer's confidence of getting honest news.

One may say that the agency's role is practically that of a transmission belt between the Party and state leadership and the media. Nevertheless, a certain formal independence from the state and the Party leaves the agency with a margin of liberty greater than that of corresponding news agencies in other Eastern countries. This relative and limited freedom, which remains dormant during times of political clampdown, could foster an evolution toward more objective news during periods of thaw.

In general, Tanjug's news policy is determined by the relationship between two forces constantly confronted within the agency: On the one hand, a relatively objective tendency based on unchanging principles of professional ethics; on the other, an attitude of political commitment and obedience to the political authorities, whose current instructions are the agency's only point of reference.

NOTES

1. La documentation francaise, "La Presse en Yougoslavie," Notes et Etudes Documentaires, no. 3, 581 (1969): 11.

2. D. Aleksic, "Tanjug: trente ans d'existence," Nouvelles Yougoslaves, no. 10 (1973): p. 6.

3. "La Presse en Yougoslavie," p. 9.

4. Ibid., p. 10.

5. Yugoslavia, Sluzebni List, no. 25 (1954).

6. Gertrude Robinson, "Tanjug: Yougoslavia's Multi-Faceted National News Agency," unpublished Ph.D. dissertation, University of Illinois, 1968, p. 58.

7. Sluzebni List, no. 12 (1962).

8. Robinson, "Tanjug," p. 174.

9. Cahiers de l'I.I.P., July/August 1969, p. 22.

10. La documentation francaise, "Le federalisme yougoslave," Notes et Etudes Documentaires, no. 3, 888-89 (1971).

11. Savezni odbor novinara Jugoslavije, Konacno izgradena fizionomija novinarske organizacije (Belgrade: Savezni odbor novinara Jugoslavije, 1971), pp. 18-20.

12. All the recent information on Tanjug in this section comes from the Yugoslav agency dispatches of June, July, and September, 1974.

13. Sluzebni List, no. 70 (1973).

14. Robinson, "Tanjug," pp. 123-24.

15. Institut yougoslave de journalisme, Presse, radio, television en Yougoslavie (Belgrade, 1966), p. 87.

17. Stjepan Pucak, "Reglement de comptes avec Confucius," Revue de politique internationale, no. 570 (1974): 25-26.

18. Vecernie Novosti, October 6, 1973.

19. Federation of Yugoslav Journalists, Bulletin (Belgrade), no. 1 (1964): 39.

20. Savezni odbor, Konacno izgradena fizionomija, p. 78.

21. Savez Novinara Jugoslavije, Srebrni Jubilej SNJ 1945-1970 (Belgrade, 1971), pp. 744-69.

The debates of the mass media section brought together about fifty scholars under the chairmanship of Georges H. Mond (Paris) and Burton Paulu (University of Minnesota). The participants heard reports by Paulu on radio and television broadcasting in Eastern Europe and by Alexandra Kwiatkowski on nonconformism in the Soviet literary press as revealed in the quarterly Novy mir. Then Georges Mink spoke about public opinion polls in the USSR and Theodore Kruglak's report on socialist news agencies was read by Helene Carrere d'Encausse of the Institut d'Etudes Politiques (Paris). Finally, Michel Kwiatkowski of Agence France-Presse (AFP) presented his report on the news policy and operation of Tanjug.

Paulu described and analyzed the theory and practice of radio and television broadcasting in the Soviet Union and in the other European socialist countries. Among the subjects covered were basic news theory, legal structure, finance, technical facilities, program objectives, audience research, and broadcasting for listeners abroad. Paulu mentioned his studies conducted during six trips to the European socialist countries and added some personal remarks on the situation in that area. Because his book Radio and Television Broadcasting in Eastern Europe has already been published (by the University of Minnesota Press and Oxford University Press, 1974), his speech is not included in this work.

Participants in the discussion that followed included the presentations of Hiromi Teratani (Hosei University, Tokyo), Abraham Brumberg (U. S. Information Agency, Washington), Elena Modrzinskaia (Institute of Philosophy of the Soviet Academy of Sciences, Moscow), and Stan Zybala (adviser to the minister of state responsible for multiculturalism, Ottawa).

Hiromi Teratani stressed that the divergent opinions in the Soviet mass media also could be found in the nonliterary press; he quoted differing opinions on the decision-making process expressed in Kommunist and Partiinaia zhizn', on management problems found in Ekonomicheskaia gazeta and Narodnoe khoziaistvo; on the models of the so-called third world in Memo and Mezhdunarodnye otnosheniia. The problem is that all these magazines and newspapers are prepared and checked by members of the Communist Party of the USSR (not the highest but quite high-ranking members of the CPSU). Therefore, it seemed to him that it is very dangerous to overestimate the nonconformist opinions expressed in Soviet magazines and newspapers. Another very important point is that it is very difficult to say, for example, whether Yevtushenko is really a conformist or.nonconformist.

Abraham Brumberg asked for some explanation about the relationship between the Novy mir team and other nonconformists. He said, "On the assumption that Novy mir represents the 'open' or 'legal' or 'loyal' opposition, can you tell us what are the relationships—political, ideological, intellectual, and personal—between the Novy mir group and the unofficial dissenters in the Soviet Union?"

Mrs. Kwiatkowski's answer to Teratani and Brumberg was:

The mobility or stability of the themes of nonconformism must not be neglected. Manifestations of nonconformism in the Soviet Union are varied, and they evolve in response to new situations, to gains or reversals in politics, economics, science, culture or ethics. The confrontations between non-conformism and conservatism could be studied in depth in various fields: philosophy, literature, law, sociology, teaching, the military. Each of the specialized magazines devoted to these questions contains specific themes and demonstrations of nonconformism at a given moment in the discussion of a problem (for example, in biology, the denunciation of Lysenkoism is no longer a theme of nonconformism; the battle has been won).

But there are also the unalterable themes, such as:

1. Anti-Stalinism in all its forms, both direct and indirect.
2. The struggle for the "authentic" truth or the "little" truth: about concentration camps, the Second World War, peasant or urban or everyday life; about science, the economy; about everything that has been deformed or camouflaged.
3. The demand for legality and for respect of the constitution and of human rights.
4. Defense of humanism and ethical values.
5. Insistence upon freedom of creation and of expression, and the struggle against censorship.

The different nonconformist, dissident, and opposition movements in the Soviet Union forge their unity around these themes. It is certain that nonconformism also exists within the Party and state apparatus, and the imporatnce of this phenomenon should not be neglected.

In the specific case of Yevtushenko and of others like him,
their position must be judged from their stand at one moment
in time.

A complete answer to Mr. Brumberg's question would require a whole thesis, but I believe that these relationships
exist, that they are complex, and that they give rise to lively
and polemical discussions, sometimes leading to fallings-
out over specific questions and situations. Divergent viewpoints in some fields, unity around other themes (for example,
what I call the unalterable themes of Soviet nonconformism);
frequent solidarity of action and, in general, mutual esteem
are all part of the relationship between the nonconformist
and the dissidents in the USSR, and among representatives
of both groups who are now abroad and whose role and impact
are of a different nature because of this fact.

Then Michel Kwiatkowski answered Stan Zybala's question about
the impact of the problem of nationalities in the work of the Yugoslav
agency Tanjug. According to Kwiatkowski, as far as it is possible to
judge from Tanjug services sent abroad, its role is to contribute to the
application of the official policy of consolidating the federation, despite
centrifugal nationalist forces, and respecting the constitutional principle
of the diversity of the five main Yugoslav nationalities. In addition, the
action of the above-mentioned centrifugal forces has had an effect on
the agency's organization, with the introduction of autonomous offices
in the federated republics.

Elena Modrzinskaia presented a long speech criticizing the reports
with the exception of Georges Mink's expose. In her comments on
Michel Kwiatkowski's report, she stressed that East European countries
are not satellites but fully independent states. Modrzinskaia said, as
far as Alexandra Kwiatkowski's report was concerned, that it was not
scientific to choose only one review and only one aspect, that of nonconformism. Then she presented a wide panorama of the rich and truthful
information published in the Soviet mass media; she stressed the character of these mass media, namely the popular and Party-guided information and comment. Modrzinskaia especially polemicized with Burton
Paulu and Alexandra Kwiatkowski; she presented a glowing image of the
Soviet mass media in answering and contesting the opinions of these
two panelists.

Modrzinskaia's 25-minute speech was the last in the debate, which
was closed by Burton Paulu. Paulu pointed out that, just as Modrzinskaia had observed that some of the points made by Alexandra Kwiatkowski and himself had emphasized only certain aspects of the problems
with which they dealt, so Modrzinskaia had selected only data that
supported her conclusions. He stated that, in order to judge the mass
media in the Soviet Union, it is necessary to look at all aspects of the
question. He said he had tried to do this but he did not feel Modrzinskaia had done so.

THE CONCEPTUAL APPROACH
TO PUBLIC OPINION
SURVEYS IN THE SOVIET UNION
Georges Mink

The ups and downs of public opinion surveys and the conceptual image of this phenomenon in the Soviet Union can only be understood through analysis of attitudes toward the phenomenon itself leaving the social and economic context altogether apart.

Numerous Soviet publications from the 1930s testify to the fact that the latent implications of conflict between the conceptual image and the phenomenon of public opinion per se were already apprehended in the Soviet Union at that time, and not always from a Marxist point of view. [1]

In a recent work furnishing results on a contemporary sociological survey on youth, S. N. Ikonnikova and V. G. Lisovskii supply some information on polls apparently initiated at the top level. [2] In spite of certain methodological weaknesses, the data confirm that the utility of social research is now recognized by central authority. [3] This constitutes a turnabout from the Stalinist period, when sociology was banned as "bourgeois and pseudo-scientific."

Until the 1960s, when revived interest in sociological research began to seep its way back to the surface as a result of de-Stalinization, the only source of data obtained was from surveys on political refugees. With the exception of the study by Inkeles and Bauer, [4] most of the surveys were carried out on limited and unrepresentative samples, of little scientific interest. [5]

The 1960s in the Soviet Union were marked by upset: a slowdown of economic growth and renewal of top power that provoked only a constrained thaw in social activity. This period has been chosen for a theoretical analysis of the problems arising out of a new approach to public opinion.

At that time attitude and market surveys carried on in the United States had furthered technical advancement in the field. J. Stoetzel

---

This essay was previously published in Revue de l'Est 6, no. 1 (1975): 207-18, and is reprinted with permission.

and A. Girard have pointed out that market analysis is in reality an anticipated form of the public opinion poll, covering consumption patterns and preferences. [6] By the same token, research on military questions was a forerunner to social research, and public opinion polls in the United States took advantage of the progress made in consumer studies. Similar circumstances bore on sociological research in Western Europe.

Economic difficulties in the Soviet Union in the 1960s also played a role in fostering the rehabilitation of empirical research and of sociology in particular. This gives credence to Rene Ahlberg's theory concerning the link between the development of public opinion polls and the will of Soviet authority to attenuate the disparity between the demand and supply of durable consumer goods in the Soviet Union. [7]

Before the economic reform in 1965, the production of durable goods was based solely on quantitative indicators. Thus, once the immediate demand is satisfied, the Soviet consumer, regardless of abundance of supply, becomes indifferent to undifferentiated merchandise because of the lack of assortment. Following this, the Soviet government found itself in 1963 faced with an unsalable stockpile evaluated at 2.5 billion rubles. [8]

This observation leads Ahlberg to assert that, in order to circumvent the plan and get a clearer view of consumer preferences, local authorities rely on market studies made at the branch level. Ahlberg's theory, however, only partially explains the origin of the sociology boom of the 1960s. Critical problems of labor productivity and work incentives were more effective in provoking sociological research and account for the importance accorded to labor sociology under the economic reform. A third factor more difficult to assess is that research in sociology affords another channel for acquiring information useful to political power.

The influence of contacts between Polish and Soviet sociologists in originating public opinion polls is rarely mentioned. While the editors of Komsomol'skaia pravda created the first institute for public opinion research in Moscow, the Polish Institute for Research on Public Opinion, attached to the radio and television services, had already been operating since 1958. It completed four studies in 1958, sixteen in 1959-60, nineteen in 1961, twenty-one in 1962, and so on. [9]

In the report on a roundtable discussion held in Moscow on November 29, 1971, with Soviet and Polish participants, the relationship of experienced colleagues to newcomers in the field is clearly expressed. J. Szczepanski drew attention to the dangers of scientific subordination to practical current interests and to the necessity of pursuing fundamental research "which sheds light on methods of concrete application and efficient practical research." He further stated: "this conference . . . enlarges our scope for developing Sociology in other Popular Democracies."[10]

Efforts to forge ahead in empirical research, as well as theoretical investigation, were confronted with conceptual ambiguity. How do you reconcile the existence of independent public opinion diverging from the one accepted by political power, while the latter's legitimacy stems

from its function as supreme representative of the historical interests
of the working class? According to uncontested principles applied under
Stalin, only a total identity of individual, collectivity, and state was
justifiable. [11] There was naturally no question of reciprocal democratic
control over the way top authority carried out its mandate. Any form of
divergence required Party intervention. Since 1960 there seems to be a
transition toward a new conception of public opinion.

It is on longer a question of holding public opinion to the rigid line
of ideological education but of determining its pattern. Ovseplian af-
firms that "our press not only expresses and molds public opinion, it
also evaluates it."[12] Thus in effect the press, via letters to the editor,
acts as the soundingboard of individual or group interests and opinions.

The same author adds that in Soviet society, where class antago-
nism has been replaced by unity of interests, proletarian psychology is
the only source from which to draw in molding public opinion. A Soviet
citizen must have the following traits: a conscientious work attitude, a
spirit of solidarity, friendship and fair play, the conviction that the
interests of society at large eclipse individual ones, patriotism, and
last but not least, internationalism. [13]

The press must therefore come up to standards. Ovseplian denounces
"anticipation" of the image of public opinion, as does R. A. Safarov,
who refers us to Lenin's thesis, "we can only govern when we correctly
express what is in the public mind."[14] Safarov asserts this emphasizes
Lenin's esteem for normal and democratic functioning of the political
apparatus and for expression of public opinion.

Why, then, these two opposed images of public opinion, which alternatively appear in Soviet texts? The explanation is in the mechanisms of social control. A more and more complex and diversified
society, whose production grew from hundreds of units in 1917 to
hundreds of thousands in 1974, can no longer count on successive in-
jections of ideological mobilization, remaining insensible to the preoccupations of social groups or individuals.

The events in Poland furnished Soviet power with a precise illustration of the risks of incompetence and social ignorance in administering
a society. The pragmatic will to know the feelings, thoughts, and desires of social groups is promising for the future of social research. It
constitutes recognition (often exercised as a contradiction or diversion
from the ideology) not only of the autonomous existence of public opinion
but also of the usefulness of studying it. Such opinions are more and
more readily expressed in the press. [15] In Zhurnalist of April 1974,
Viktoriia Siradze, Secretary of the Central Committee of the Georgian
Communist Party, underlined the importance of the press as the echo of
public opinion by coverage of a sort of local "Watergate" that brought
about the dismissal of those involved. [16] She affirmed that Party organizations in the Georgian Republic had to exert every effort to compel re-
porters to publicize the problems on which men's work and lives
depend. [17]

The same idea is developed at length by I. Klimenko in an article on Party organizations and the shaping of public opinion. [18] For this author, public opinion constitutes the essence of the relationship of social groups or classes to the workings of social life. In the socialist context, where class differences have disappeared, social, political and ideological unity (the three social factors) should serve as a touchstone for public opinion. Party organizations should not conjecture about or impose public opinion but offer the framework for apprehending it. Dissent in public opinion should find channels for unity of expression within the Party. (Diversity of public opinion finds representation in the local soviets, where 14,000 deputies and 200,000 militants participate.)[19] But the Party is not a sufficient framework for a global comprehension of opinion and should be supported by sociological research that has already proved its effectiveness. Investigation should be carried as far as possible to aid the Party in shaping public opinion. [20]

In this seemingly double-negative approach in which public opinion is only theoretically liberated from its dependence on higher authority,[21] there is still room for a large degree of autonomy and the road is clear for empirical research. [22]

Recent encouragement will probably reanimate Soviet sociology, which appears either to have been subsisting since 1968 on findings from previous investigations or shielding itself from attacks by reverting to criticism of bourgeois sociology and occidental analysis. [23]

The trend in Soviet sociology is toward almost parallel studies on public opinion, using both empirical and theoretical methods. Uledov, in an inquiry on public opinion entitled "A Study of the Social Conscience in Soviet Society," admits to the empirical discovery of the heterogeneous character of public opinion and the ideological necessity of identity of purpose within the Party, the collective, and for the individual. He regrets what he refers to as the "positivistic" or "equalitarian" conception of public opinion—and more specifically the choice of samples based on such criteria as age and sex without distinguishing among social groups as carriers of ideological opinions.

Uledov favors research in social psychology and observes, for example, that a speech delivered with fire unifies the group and stimulates the decision-making process. However, he approves of manipulation of opinion, [24] and to put an end to this dilemma introduces the concept of "socialist public," somewhere midway between individual divergence of opinion and conformity to ideology.

B. A. Grushin goes much farther, in particular in relation to empirical investigation. During the five years in which his institute functioned, twelve studies were made on the following themes:

1. Can humanity prevent war? (May 1960)
2. In what way has your standard of living changed? (1960)
3. What do you think of your generation? (1961)
4. What do you think about planning for the future? (1961)

5. What do you think about young couples? (December 1963)
6. What do words signify? (January 1962)
7. Where will studies lead you? (1962)
8. How do you spend free time? (1963)
9. To Mars—with what? (1963)
10. Let's do the planning ourselves (July 1964)
11. An invention in search of a name (1964-65)
12. Are you satisfied with your lot? (November 1965).[25]

Using questioning techniques imported from the United States, the surveys presented a certain guarantee of representativity. And although the results of these inquiries altered readymade ideas about the Soviet man-in-the-street's conception of life, both in the Soviet Union and in the West, they were somewhat the reverse of what might have been expected, if any assessment can be made of the surface value of the titles of these studies, which appear in themselves rather revolutionary. On the whole, the data seemed to confirm Inkeles's theory that ideological unity exists for the Soviet citizen and that his system of values is assimilated in such a way as to make it difficult to construct an "anti" public opinion grounded on empirical Soviet findings.[26]

In the Soviet Union, however, the diversity of public opinion, the vision of a population with its own views, feelings, desires, scale of values (granted a small percentage, but significant) was a stupefying revelation.

In the study entitled "What do you think of your generation?" a sample of 17,446 persons (aged 14 to 30) representing the spectrum of social groups was interrogated.[27] The question, "What is the characteristic trait of soviet youth?" obtained the following responses, in order of preference:

1. Patriotism
2. Moral superiority—will, courage, love of truth, feelings for others
3. Fidelity to the Party and communist ideals
4. Thirst for knowledge
5. Love of work
6. Spirit of cooperation
7. Enthusiasm and adaptability
8. Desire for change
9. Love of peace
10. Internationalism.[28]

Facing distinct signs of variance of public opinion, some analysts have spoken of a synchronization of public opinion, as opposed to the idea of unity of opinion. (The idea behind this seems to be to synchronize the differences.[29])

For example, 11 percent of those questioned indicated dissatisfaction with their generation. On these grounds, advocates of the "Marxist" conception of public opinion started clamoring for the intensification of ideological instruction. (It seems worth noting that although unified public opinion was clearly absent, an attitude of conformity or lack of interest is visible from the general order of preference in the responses.)

In the presence of steadily increasing empirical material, Grushin could propose that Uledov's concept of a socialist public, a total consensus of opinion, being applicable only to certain problems and under certain conditions, then public opinion must henceforth be considered as a product of the conscience of different social groups.[30] Researchers should study not only public opinion but also the social strata of the persons expressing it and the object it reflects or represents.[31]

In spite of the obstacles and incoherences, surveys and studies of public opinion are progressing. The Institute of Sociological Research of the USSR Academy of Sciences, directed by Professor M. N. Rutkevich, corresponding member of the Academy of Sciences, employs nearly 400 sociologists.[32] The problems under consideration include theories and methodology for social planning, particular attention being devoted to predictions and the study of public opinion (100 collaborators), and programming and organizing public opinion polls. The political sociologist Professor F. M. Burlatskii and B. A. Grushin, who heads the mass media section of the Institute of Sociology, are particularly interested in research on the influence of mass media on attitudes.

Using Western methodology, the Center for Studies in Sociology in Novosibirsk has already completed several surveys, including an analysis of the contents of such newspapers as Literaturnaia gazeta, Trud, and Pravda as well as analysis of readers' opinions. A special seminar was held in Novosibirsk devoted to the analysis of Western techniques and entitled "The Problems of Content Analysis in Sociology."[33]

In conclusion, two observations come to mind:

1. If we place ourselves in the optimistic current of Sovietology, it seems evident that Soviet society, as well as those of the People's Democracies, has attained a cultural and technological level in this field comparable to that of modern industrial societies. In this context, sociological research and especially public opinion polls are necessary to political power. There is increasing pressure to give due consideration to the link between holding power and the opinion of those under it.

A student of Soviet sociology is tempted to wonder whether publicized results are not limited only to those that top authority wishes to communicate. An example is a study made to celebrate the fiftieth anniversary of Izvestiia. Some 25,000 questionnaires were sent to subscribers. The editor-in-chief made some comments on percentages and promised full publication of the results at a later date. But that was in in 1967.[34]

2. Supposing that administration needs to know the society it governs, partisans of the distinction between the concept of "public opinion" and "class consciousness" or "national conscience" are holding a trump card: the operational effectiveness of the division of

precepts backed up by advanced research techniques. Analysis of Soviet surveys makes it possible to conclude that once again diffusion of
techniques precedes the implementation of ideological adaptation.

NOTES

1. V. Kuz'michev, Organizatsiia obshchestvennogo mneniia (Moscow and Leningrad: Gosudarstvennoe izdatel'stvo, 1929); V. M. Bekh-
terev, Kollektivnaia refleksologiia (Petrograd: Kolos, 1921).

2. S. N. Ikonnikova and V. G. Lisovskii, Molodezh' o sebe, o
svoikh sverstnikakh (Sotsiologicheskoe issledovanie) (Leningrad:
Leninzdat, 1969).

3. A study on attitudes to Soviet authority was carried out in 1927
by A Zalkind to determine the influence of the Revolution on the conscience of the younger generation. Zalkind's sample was composed of
adolescents aged 10 to 16. Four years previously, N. Poznanskii had
done a study on the image of the hero, and in 1929 researchers at the
Economic Institute of Pedagogy made an inquiry on young workers in the
K. Marx factories in Leningrad. (See Ikonnikova and Lisovskii, Molodezh', pp. 21-33.)

4. A. Inkeles and R. Bauer, The Soviet Citizen: Daily Life in a
Totalitarian Society (Cambridge, Mass.: Harvard University Press,
1959).

5. Cf. S. White, "Communist Political Culture: An Empirical Note,"
Newsletter on Comparative Studies of Communism 6, no. 2 (1973): 41-
45. White quotes, among others, Solomon's study, Mao's Revolution
and the Chinese Political Culture (Berkeley, Calif.: University of California Press, 1971), which bases generalizations about the political
culture in China on interviews of 91 immigrants while the population of
China is 700 million.

6. J. Stoetzel and A. Girard, Les sondages d'opinion publique
(Paris: Presses Universitaires de France, 1973), p. 48.

7. R. Ahlberg, "Offentliche Meinung und Meinungsforschung in
der UdSSR," Osteuropa 19, no. 3 (1969): 168.

8. Ia. Orlov, "Vzaimootnosheniia mezhdu promyshlennost'iu i
torgovlei," Voprosy ekonomiki, no. 11 (1964): 113.

9. Cf. Andrzej Sicinski, ed., Spoleczenstwo polskie w badaniach
ankietowych (Warsaw: PWN, 1966).

10. J. Szczepanski, "Konferencja socjologow w Moskwie. Kronike
zycia naukowego," Studia Socjologiczne 2, no. 1 (1962): 286. The eminent position of Polish scientists can doubtless be attributed in part to
the importance of the Polish October in 1956, but also to the presence
of a cohesive school of sociological thought whose adherents, many of
whom already had an international reputation, were, after a short period
of eclipse in 1948-50, rehabilitated to direct the laboratories and form
research groups.

11. Ahlberg, "Offentliche Meinung," p. 162.

12. R. P. Ovseplian, "Obshchestvennoe mnenie i pechat'," Vestnik Moskovskogo Universiteta, 11th series Zhurnalistika 21, no. 4 (1966): 13-22, reviewed in G. Mond, "Opinion publique et la presse en URSS," Canadian Slavonic Papers 10, no. 3 (1968): 385-94.

13. G. Mond, "Opinion publique," p. 387. Mond makes the following comment: "Thus the Soviet press follows the line of historical materialism, attributing the principal role in the process of forming public opinion to the Communist Party of the USSR."

14. R. A. Safarov, "Vyiavlenie obshchestvennogo mneniia v gosudarstvenno-pravovoi praktike," Sovetskoe gosudarstvo i pravo, no. 10 (1967): 46-55.

15. Armed intervention by the Warsaw Pact countries in Czechoslovakia coincided, however, with a freeze on sociological publications.

16. Viktoriia Siradze, "Atakuiushchee slovo pravdy," Zhurnalist, no. 4 (1974): 5-7.

17. Ibid., p. 7.

18. I. Klimenko, "Partiinye organizatsii i formirovanie obshchestvennogo mneniia," Kommunist 51, no. 4 (1974): 15-26. In the text, the three elements of society are the workers, farmers, and intellectuals (Ibid., p. 15).

19. Ibid., p. 21.

20. Ibid., p. 26.

21. S. M. Gurevich in his book on the theory of information, Problemy informatsii v pechati (Ocherki teorii i praktiki) (Moscow: Mysl', 1971), suggests a schema for the circulation of information where public opinion is entirely rehabilitated to an autonomous function and proposes the following outline: world goals (nature, society); public opinion (as a means of assimilation); ideology (the sphere of social conscience); communication (here choice depends on the ideological position); the channel (ways and means of informing); information flow; and reception.

22. The dual approach to public opinion remains present investigations but is expressed by commentaries (or the absence of them), but this still leaves room for concrete findings to speak for themselves. For example, in one of the most recent studies effected in Hungary on political attitudes of Hungarian workers, the following question was asked: "What in your opinion is the principle on which relations between socialist countries are based?" Some 47 percent responded "internationalism," and 50 percent "peaceful coexistence." The authors considered that internationalism was the correct answer. The same was true of the question "Who is waging war in Vietnam?" Some 23 percent answered that no party was waging a just war. This answer was marked incorrect in Delmagyarorszag, February 6, 1972, p. 7.

23. Cf. M. T. Iovchuk and L. N. Kogan, eds. Dukhovyi mir sovetskogo rabochego: opyt konkretno-sotsiologicheskogo issledovaniia (Moscow: Mysl', 1972). In exposing the results of an inquiry carried on in 1968-71 in the Ural factories, the book disagrees with Western

sociologists and tries to prove that the degree of participation of Soviet workers in public life is one of the highest in the world.

24. A. K. Uledov, Obshchestvennoe mnenie sovetskogo obshchestva (Moscow: Sotsekgiz, 1963).

25. B. A. Grushin, Mnenie o mire i mir mnenii (Moscow: Politizdat, 1967), p. 13.

26. Inkeles and Bauer, The Soviet Citizen.

27. B. A. Grushine, "Regards vers l'avenir: Resultats d'un son-dage," Problemes de la paix et du socialisme, no. 10 (1962): 840; B. A. Grushin and V. Chikin, Ispoved' pokoleniia (Moscow: Molodaia gvardiia, 1962).

28. Even if some criticism were made of the methods employed and the enlargement of the sample, these results are confirmed by all the youth surveys. Cf. Ikonnikova and Lisovskii, Molodezh', as well as V. N. Shubkin's study in Novosibirsk, "Molodezh' vstupaiet v zhizn'," Voprosy filosofii 19, no. 5 (1965): 57-70, and M. N. Rutkevich, ed., Zhiznennye plany molodezhi (Ural'skii gos universitet im. Gor'kogo, Sotsiologicheskie issledovaniia, Vyp. 1, Sverdlovsk, 1966).

29. Ahlberg, "Offentliche Meinung."

30. Grushine, "Regards vers l'avenir."

31. A. V. Prigozhin, "Metodologicheskie problemy issledovaniia obshchestvennogo mneniia," Voprosy filosofii, no. 2 (1969): pp. 67-73.

32. Cf. J. Darmo, "Novinovedny vyskum vZSSR," Otazky Zhurnal-istyki, no. 1 (1971): 50-52, and in Problemy sotsiologii pechati v 3-kh vyp. Vyp. 1: Istoriia. Metodologiia. Metodika (Novosibirsk: Nauka, Sibirskoe otdelenie, 1971).

33. For recent information, see "Le rapport de la mission francaise: La sociologie en URSS," Revue Francaise de sociologie 14, no. 3 (1973): 396-409.

34. About this survey, see Zycie Warszawy, August 8, 1967; Polityka, August 19, 1967, p. 2; Kommunist 43, no. 1 (1967): 73-84; Izvestiia, March 14, 1967; and Le Monde, March 16, 1967, p. 4.

9

CONCLUSION
Bohdan Harasymiw

Although the essays in this volume were not originally written with a common purpose in mind, they do nevertheless contribute to the illumination of certain themes. They also contribute an interdisciplinary understanding of the subject of education and the mass media in the Soviet Union and East Europe. Beyond this, their authors raise some questions of fundamental importance regarding the relationship between public policy and ideas in general, as well as in communist systems in particular.

What are these themes and questions? Obviously, in a work such as this the common ground should be sought at the philosophical level, for none of the authors has made deliberate efforts to link his chapter to the others. Yet it is possible to discern these theoretical threads, which run through their writing.

One is a basic question as to the purpose of public education. Whose interests is it to serve—the state's? The individual's? The society's? Naturally, it must be some combination of the three. But there is no easy formula, and no guarantee that the benefit of one is not bought at the expense of another, or that a particular policy will not be self-defeating. It seems to me that the Soviet case examined here clearly shows this. It also shows that the Soviet government's control of educational policy is slipping, that individual and social interests are overtaking those of the state in its formulation. So that ideas (among the public) are having an effect on policy affecting ideas. And the teleological question regarding public education is also surfacing there.

In a similar vein, politicians as well as students of comparative education in both East and West are asking about the relationship between education and society. What is the relationship? What should it be? How is the kind of education to be matched with the kind of society that exists or may be desired?

Such questions lead one to identify the second major theme in this volume, namely, the production of intellectuals and their role in the sociopolitical system. Several of the essays deal at least implicitly with the problems of opinion formation and of the relationship between intellectuals and masses. One explores the subject of communication among intellectuals. Together, they point to a significant research problem: Does the production of more intellectuals lead to the secularization of a society's political culture?

If one were to summarize the findings of our authors, as opposed to the theoretical themes, I think they could be subsumed under three headings: comparability, change and interdisciplinary study. It is quite obvious that socialist and nonsocialist systems are comparable, and that study of the former should not be circumscribed by ideological boundaries. The problems of the relationships between politicians on the one hand and educators, students, intellectuals, and journalists on the other are comparable across ideological borders. If there is analytically such a thing as a communist political system (as opposed to a general political system by means of which knowledge of politics can be scientifically pursued), these essays indicate that it may be defined by the relative political subordination of education, information, and opinion. They suggest, in other words, that a politically controlled political culture may be a crucial defining characteristic of a communist system, analytically speaking. That, at any rate, is what a political scientist carries away from the volume.

The second important finding here is change. This is twofold: There is change apparent in the sociopolitical systems under study, and there is change in the field of comparative study of these systems. Communist studies are broadening. Even when the subject is a fairly narrow case study, one cannot help but see the broader implications. Scholars are less satisfied with the area approach. Broader comparison appears more fruitful.

Finally, I think the essays, although they do not undertake it themselves, point out the need for the development of interdisciplinary study. Even though they have not done so, it seems beyond debate that the reader will have acquired a deeper appreciation of the subject of public policy and ideas through their multidisciplinary approaches. A further challenge is for scholars to explore more fully the same subject, but through the self-conscious use of interdisciplinary techniques. Such techniques would seem the most suitable for the study of public policy questions such as the following, which I believe are raised in this volume.

How do governments discern society's needs? Whose needs are being met by government policy—the government's or society's? What are the respective needs of society and of the nation-state? What are the limits of public policy? Do governments in the Soviet Union and Eastern Europe fear ideas? Do unofficial ideas nevertheless have an impact on public policy? If so, the explanation of political change in these countries must be sought in change of political culture, in the broadening of acceptable ideas.

OSKAR ANWEILER is Professor in the Institut fur Padagogik at the Ruhr University in Bochum and is author of <u>Geschichte der Schule und Pada-gogik in Russland</u> (1964), <u>Die Ratebewegung in Russland, 1905-1921</u> (1958), and <u>Die Sowjetpadagogik in der Welt von reute</u> (1968), and has contributed to Richard Pipes, ed., <u>Revolutionary Russia</u> (1967).

GEORGE AVIS, Lecturer in Russian Studies at the University of Brad-ford, England, and former editor of the <u>Journal of Russian Studies</u>, is interested in Soviet and Yugoslav education.

BOHDAN HARASYMIW, Associate Professor of Political Science at the University of Calgary, contributed the chapter on the USSR in <u>Post-Secondary Education in a Technological Society</u>, edited by T. H. McLeod (1973).

ELISABETH KOUTAISSOFF is presently living in Oxford. She was for-merly senior lecturer at the University of Birmingham (England), and Professor of Russian at Victoria University, Wellington, New Zealand. Her book <u>The Soviet Union</u> appeared in the series <u>Nations of the Modern World</u> in 1971.

THEODORE E. KRUGLAK is Professor of Journalism at the University of Southern California, has won numerous awards for journalism research, has been Fulbright Professor at Rome and Ankara, and is probably best known for his book, <u>The Two Faces of TASS</u>.

ALEXANDRA KWIATKOWSKI did her doctoral work in Paris on aspects of nonconformism in the Soviet literary press and has contributed to <u>Le Monde</u>, <u>L'Exil</u> (Geneva), and <u>Revista Espanola de la Opinion Publica</u> (Madrid).

MICHEL KWIATKOWSKI is a graduate of Warsaw University and the Institut Francais de Presse et des Sciences de l'Information (Paris II University) and works as a journalist with Agence France-Presse.

GEORGES MINK is a lecturer in sociology at Rene Descartes Univer-sity in Paris. He is currently writing a study on the relationship between the intelligentsia and political power in Eastern Europe.

GEORGES H. MOND lectures at Paris II University and conducts re-search at the Centre National de la Recherche Scientifique. He was for-merly deputy director of the Polish Press Institute and secretary general of the Polish Union of Journalists.

I. Volumes in the Social Sciences, published by Praeger Publishers,
    Praeger Special Studies, New York:

    Economic Development in the Soviet Union and Eastern Europe:
    Reforms, Technology, and Income Distribution, edited by Zbigniew
    M. Fallenbuchl, University of Windsor.

    Economic Development in the Soviet Union and Eastern Europe:
    Sectoral Analysis, edited by Zbigniew M. Fallenbuchl, University
    of Windsor.

    Education and the Mass Media in the Soviet Union and Eastern
    Europe, edited by Bohdan Harasymiw, University of Calgary.

    Soviet Economic and Political Relations with the Developing World,
    edited by Roger E. Kanet and Donna Bahry, University of Illinois,
    Urbana-Champaign.

    Demographic Developments Eastern Europe, edited by Leszek
    Kosinski, University of Alberta.

    Problems of Environmental Misuse in the Soviet Union, edited by
    Fred Singleton, University of Bradford.

    Change and Adaptation in Soviet and East European Politics, edited
    by Jane P. Shapiro, Manhattanville College, and Peter J. Potichnyj,
    McMaster University.

    From the Cold War to Dentente, edited by Peter J. Potichnyj,
    McMaster University, and Jane P. Shapiro, Manhattanville College.

II. Volumes in the Humanities, published by Slavica Publishers, Cam-
    bridge, Mass.:

    Russian and Slavic Literature to 1917, edited by Richard Freeborn,
    University of London, and Charles A. Ward, University of Wiscon-
    sin, Milwaukee.

    Russian and Slavic Literature, 1917-1974, edited by Robin Milner-
    Gulland, University of Sussex, and Charles A. Ward, University
    of Wisconsin, Milwaukee.

Slavic Linguistics at Banff, edited by Thomas F. Magner, Pennsylvania State University.

Early Russian History, edited by G. Edward Orchard, University of Lethbridge.

Nineteenth and Twentieth Century Slavic History, edited by Don Karl Rowney, Bowling Green State University.

Reconsiderations on the Russian Revolution, edited by Carter Elwood, Carleton University.

III.   Additional Volumes:

"Nomads and the Slavic World," a special issue of AEMAe Archivum Eurasiae Medii Aevi, 2 (1975), edited by Tibor Halasi-Kun, Columbia University.

Russian Literature in the Age of Catherine the Great: A Collection of Essays. Oxford: Willem A. Meeuws, 1976, edited by Anthony Cross, University of East Anglia.

Commercial and Legal Problems in East-West Trade. Ottawa: Carleton University, Russian and East European Center, 1976, edited by John P. Hardt, U.S. Library of Congress.

Marxism and Religion in Eastern Europe. Dordrecht and Boston: D. Reidel, 1976, edited by Richard T. DeGeorge, University of Kansas, and James P. Scanlan, The Ohio State University.

Detente and the Conference on Security and Cooperation in Europe. Leiden: Sythoff, 1976, edited by Louis J. Mensonides, Virginia Polytechnic Institute and State University.